DATE DUE

GUYANA

Leslie Jermyn

MARSHALL CAVENDISH
New York • London • Sydney

Reference edition reprinted 2001 by
Marshall Cavendish Corporation
99 White Plains Road
Tarrytown
New York 10591

Originated and designed by
Times Books International, an imprint of
Times Media Private Limited, a member of the
Times Publishing Group

Printed in Malaysia

Library of Congress Cataloging-in-Publication Data:

Jermyn, Leslie.
    Guyana / Leslie Jermyn.
        p. cm. — (Cultures of the world)
    Includes bibliographical references (p.) and index.
    Summary: Examines the geography, history, government,
    economy, people, and culture of Guyana.
    ISBN 0-7614-0994-7 (lib. bdg.)
    1. Guyana—Juvenile literature. [1. Guyana.] I. Title.
II. Series.

F2368.5 .J47 2000
988.1—dc21   99-055063
                    CIP
                    AC

INTRODUCTION

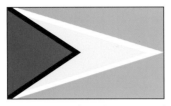

TWO WORDS CHARACTERIZE GUYANA—diverse and unique. Guyana is the only English-speaking country in South America. It is also one of the few countries in the world in which the indigenous population is growing in numbers. Its history has produced these anomalies along with an incredible diversity of cultures, religions, and lifestyles, ranging from tropical urban living to roughing it in the wild prospecting for gold and diamonds. Diversity is also apparent in its geographic and natural environment.

In this book, we will learn about all of these things and more. We'll begin by setting the scene with geography and history, then move on to government and the economy. From there, we will turn to the people of Guyana and learn about their lifestyles, languages, religions, arts, festivals and foods. Get ready to be surprised by the complexity and beauty of all that is Guyana!

CONTENTS

Guyanese fishermen with their catch.

CONTENTS

An East Indian woman selling eggs in a market.

GEOGRAPHY

THE COOPERATIVE REPUBLIC OF GUYANA ("gy-AN-uh"), or Guyana for short, is one of three small countries located in the northeast of the South American continent. It has an area of 83,000 square miles (214,969 square km), about the same size as Great Britain or Idaho. Guyana lies between 1° and 9° north latitude and 57° and 61° west longitude. It borders Venezuela to the west, Brazil to the west and south, Suriname to the east, and the Atlantic Ocean to the north.

The capital city, Georgetown, is located on the Atlantic coast. Guyana is a tropical country with rainy and dry seasons, and minor seasonal temperature change. Several important rivers flow across a land rich in plant and animal life.

Opposite: **The spectacular 822-foot (250-m) high Kaieteur Falls on the Potaro River.**

Left: **Sugarcane fields southwest of Georgetown.**

Apart from infertile soils, the main reason people do not want to live in the highlands is the lack of transportation and services.

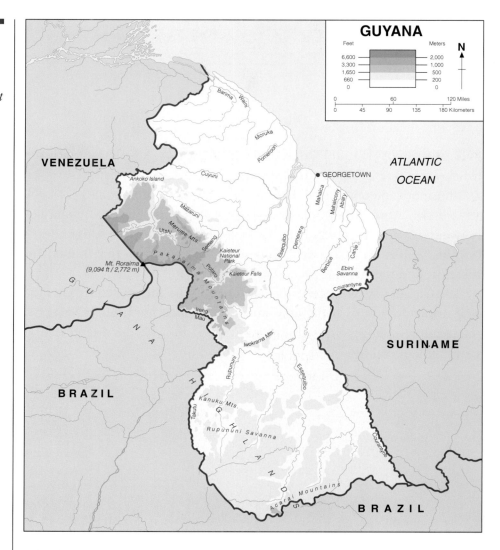

GEOGRAPHIC REGIONS

Guyana is part of a large region known as the Guianas ("gee-AH-nahs"), which includes eastern Venezuela, northern Brazil, Suriname, and French Guiana. The region is characterized by great river systems and high annual rainfall. Four main natural and climatic zones can be distinguished within Guyana's boundaries—the coast, the forests, the savanna, and the mountains.

THE COASTAL ZONE This is the narrow strip of land bordering the Atlantic Ocean where most of Guyana's economic activities take place. The coastal zone stretches 270 miles (435 km) from Venezuela to Suriname and varies in width from 10 miles (16 km) up to 40 miles (64 km) along major rivers. Although this zone represents only 4% of total land area, it is very fertile. Thus it is where most Guyanese live and where the two main crops, sugar and rice, are grown.

It is bordered by the ocean on one side and swamps inland, making it very susceptible to floods. Some of this area would normally lie 4 to 5 feet (1.2 to 1.5 m) below sea level but is protected by a complicated system of dikes and seawalls. The coastal zone also has high annual rainfall of 80–110 inches (203–297 cm), which further increases the chances of flooding.

Bartica on the Essequibo River seen from the air.

THE FOREST ZONE Covering over 66,000 square miles (170,940 square km), the forest zone makes up the largest portion of the country and stretches from the coastal zone to the interior. As the name implies, it is heavily forested. Few people live here as the soil, made up of brown and white sands and clays, is not suitable for cultivating food crops. The land in this zone rises gently from sea level, and the area is crisscrossed with large rivers that empty into the Atlantic Ocean.

The four largest rivers in Guyana are the Demerara, Essequibo, Berbice, and Courantyne. As these rivers flow from their sources high in the mountains to the ocean, the shift in altitude results in dramatic rapids, cataracts, and waterfalls. Guyana has some of the continent's most spectacular waterfalls, and these are popular tourist destinations.

STAYING DRY ON THE COAST

The densely settled and farmed coastal strip is sandwiched between the Atlantic Ocean on one side and swamps on the other. Much of this land lies below sea level. In order to keep the land dry, the Guyanese have constructed and maintained a complicated system of walls, sluices, and canals to control flooding.

The first part of the system is a large seawall that prevents the sea from flooding this part of the shore. The wall is equipped with sluices that regulate the outflow of water back to the sea and from inland swamps to the sea. At the rear of the coastal strip is another wall or dam that prevents swamp water from flooding the settled zone. Between these two dams is a complex network of canals and trenches that move water through the area for irrigation and drainage.

The canals and trenches are of two different levels. The high canals are used for irrigation and transportation, while the low trenches are for drainage. These canals and trenches must be kept clean of silt (fine sand that can clog water systems) and plants. Maintaining the system is the responsibility of both the government and the people. The Public Works Department undertakes major repairs to the canals and trenches, but local communities are responsible for maintaining the sluices and cleaning the canals of plant life. Without hard work and cooperation, life on the coast would be impossible.

THE SAVANNA ZONE This is an area of high grasslands located in the far southwest of the country near the border with Brazil. The largest savanna area is called Rupununi, after the river by the same name that runs through the region. Totaling about 6,000 square miles (15,540 square km), the Rupununi Savanna is divided in half by the Kanuku Mountains.

The area is sparsely settled, although some Guyanese have cattle ranches there and a few indigenous groups make their homes on the savanna. There is a second, smaller savanna near the mouth of the Berbice River. Called the Ebini Savanna, it has an area of about 2,000 square miles (5,180 square km).

MAGNIFICENT WATERFALLS

Guyana boasts of some of the highest and most beautiful waterfalls in the world. Kaieteur Falls, on the Potaro River, is a spectacular 822 feet (250 m) high. It consists of two falls, a small one of 81 feet (25 m) and a larger one of 741 feet (225 m). By comparison, Niagara Falls is only 193 feet (59 m) high. Kaieteur Falls is a major tourist attraction because of its sheer size and the beautiful prismatic colors that form with the mist rising off the water. It is also home to martins and swallows that nest behind the curtain of water; they can be seen swooping home after foraging for food in the surrounding forests.

The name Kaieteur comes from an indigenous language and means "Old Man's Fall." Legend has it that an old chieftain offered himself to the Great Spirit for the good of his people. He paddled his canoe over the edge of the falls and was turned to stone. It is said that you can see his stone canoe when there is a drought and the water level is low. Despite the magnificent size of Kaieteur, it is not the biggest waterfall in Guyana. Two falls are higher—King George VI Falls on the Utshi River at 1,600 feet (488 m) and King Edward Falls on the Semang River at 840 feet (256 m). However, these are not popular tourist attractions because they are hard to reach. Many of Guyana's rivers have smaller falls and rapids that are more accessible from the coast, such as Orinduik Falls (see photo) on the Ireng River at the Brazilian border.

MYSTERIOUS RORAIMA

Mount Roraima is actually a *mesa* ("MAY-sah") or plateau, rather than a mountain. It is part of a vast 200,000-square-mile (518,000-square-km) region of sandstone *mesas* that cover the western bulge of Guyana (above the "waist" where the country narrows) and parts of Venezuela and Brazil. These plateaus are what remain of a large sandstone deposit that covered this region 1.8 billion years ago. The rock is so old that it predates the time when South America and Africa parted to form separate continents 135 million years ago.

Over the millennia, water erosion from many rivers has carved deep ravines and valleys into the *mesas*. Roraima is the highest of the plateaus. Its name in a native language means "singing of waterfalls," which is an apt description, as there are many streams of water plunging off its edges to the lowlands below. This region is mostly unexplored because of the difficult terrain.

The first expedition to reach the top of Roraima was led by Everard Im Thurn, a British botanist, in 1884. Im Thurn brought back samples of plant life that had never been recorded before. The plateaus are isolated because of their height, and this has allowed plants and animals to evolve and thrive in an ecological niche not found anywhere else in the world.

There is even one species of toad that is related to a species in Africa, suggesting that there was once a common ancestor for both when the continents were joined. This toad, *Oreophrynella quelchii*, has not needed to evolve much in this isolated environment and can neither hop nor swim. When Im Thurn lectured on this isolated region on his return to England, Arthur Conan Doyle (the creator of Sherlock Holmes) was inspired to write a novel about an expedition in which prehistoric plants and dinosaurs are discovered living high up on Roraima. The book, called *The Lost World*, was published in 1912.

Today, even with modern technology such as helicopters, much of Roraima's 44 square miles (114 square km) remains unexplored.

THE MOUNTAINOUS ZONE Along the borders with Venezuela and Brazil are the Pakaraima Mountains. This area is characterized by sharply-stepped plateaus rising from the savanna plains below. It is the least settled and least known region of Guyana. There are believed to be some gold and diamond deposits in the mountains, but due to the lack of transportation, few people from the coast have made the journey to try their luck.

The highest point in this range, and in Guyana, is Mount Roraima at 9,094 feet (2,772 m) high. It is located at the point where Venezuela, Brazil, and Guyana meet. Other mountain ranges in Guyana include the Kanuku Mountains and the Merume Mountains.

CLIMATE

As Guyana is situated close to the equator, temperatures are high throughout the year. The average daily temperature is 80°F (27°C), with a range of 75°F to 88°F (24°C to 31°C) between night and day. For most people living on the coast, these temperatures are moderated by the constant northeast trade winds blowing off the Atlantic Ocean.

Four seasons, defined by the amount of rainfall, can be distinguished in Guyana. From mid-April to mid-August there is heavy rainfall. This is followed by a dry season to mid-November, when another period of lighter rainfall begins. This third season lasts until mid-February when there is another dry season.

The average annual rainfall in Guyana is 90 inches (228 cm), with a range from a low of 60 inches (152 cm) to a high of 120 inches (304 cm), depending on the area and the year. Even during the dry season, however, the humidity in the air is very high, averaging about 80%. This watery climate has influenced many aspects of life in Guyana, including dress, the design of houses, and the annual cycle of social events.

Anthills in Rupununi Savanna.

PLANTS AND ANIMALS

Guyana boasts of an extraordinary diversity in plant and animal life. From the sea to the deep Amazon regions, there are different ecosystems supporting many different trees, plants, insects, reptiles, amphibians, fish, and mammals.

13

Regis water lilies grow-
ing in the Rupununi
River.

There are three principal types of forest in Guyana—mangrove, hardwood, and tropical. Mangrove forests grow along the boundary between fresh and salt water and survive in a mixture of the two known as brine. Mangroves can be found behind the settled coastal band in the swampy areas where rivers drain into the sea. From there, inland to the first line of cataracts on the major rivers, lies hardwood forest. Forest trees have adapted to living in sandy soil by extending their roots outward to capture water. Tropical forests extend from the cataracts to the border with Brazil and Venezuela. These are dense forests that have largely escaped commercial logging because of their isolation. Some of the species that can be found there include greenheart, mora, and crabwood. These trees can grow to hundreds of feet. Greenheart is especially valuable because its wood does not rot in sea water and can be used to build docks and wharves.

Notable smaller plants include hundreds of varieties of orchids, some of which have adapted to living in trees with no soil, and the Regis water

UNDERWATER WORLD

One of the inhabitants of Guyana's rivers is a fish seven feet (2 m) long and weighing 200 pounds (90 kg). This is the famous arapaima ("ah-rah-PAI-mah"), a freshwater fish related to the salmon. The arapaima inhabit rivers in the highlands and savannas and are sought by indigenous people and sportsmen alike. They are hunted with harpoons rather than lines and hooks because the fish is so big and strong, it can drag a fisherman off the bank of a river. Another freshwater giant is the caiman. This reptile is related to the crocodile and alligator and can grow up to 10 feet (3 m) in length.

The anaconda is a type of boa constrictor that prefers to live partly in water. These giants can easily crush a human being, although their usual prey is large animals. Many of the water inhabitants are huge. The manatee or sea cow (see photo) is a mammal that breathes air through collapsible nostrils and suckles its live-born babies, but never leaves the rivers. A manatee eats only plants and is a docile creature. Measuring up to seven feet (2 m) in length, manatees are probably the inspiration for the mermaid myths started by sailors hundreds of years ago.

Another river inhabitant is the capybara ("kah-pee-BAH-rah") or water pig. The world's largest rodent, it is the size of a small pig. It lives near water and can be found there for much of the day. Indigenous people hunt capybaras for their meat. The matamata ("MAH-tah-mah-tah") turtle lives in rivers and hunts fish by luring them with strange weed-like appendages on its head. A species of eel that carries 500 watts of electric current also inhabits Guyana's waterways.

lily, which lives in freshwater pools. This water lily is the largest leafed aquatic plant in the world and it is claimed that it can support the weight of a 5-year-old child without sinking. In the tropical jungle, one can find several types of vines that live suspended from huge trees. The most well-known of these is the liana ("lee-AH-nah") vine, which is a weak tree that grows up the trunk of another in search of sunlight. The bark of a different

Above: **The macaw is one the many beautiful birds found in the forests of Guyana.**

Opposite: **A street near the waterfront in George-town.**

vine, known locally as urari ("oo-RAH-ree"), is used to make a poison that is more deadly than that of many snakes.

As a tropical country, Guyana also has many insects, including beautiful jungle butterflies such as the Morpho butterfly and leaf-cutter ants. The leaf-cutter or parasol ant is a species that grows a type of fungus for food in its underground nests. The fungus needs rotting vegetation to survive, so the leaf-cutters work hard to provide their food with food. They can strip a tree of leaves very quickly.

With so many rivers, it is no surprise that Guyana has an abundance of freshwater fish. The most famous Amazon fish is perhaps the piranha ("pee-RAH-nah"), with its sharp teeth and carnivorous habits. Some species of piranhas attack humans and other large mammals, but most species are not meat-eaters. They also prefer still pools of water, so many rapids and waterfalls in Guyana are safe. A favorite with sport fishermen is the lukanani ("loo-kah-NAH-nee"), which resembles the large mouth bass. Another member of Guyana's diverse fish life is the arapaima, which can grow to 200 pounds (90 kg).

Bird life includes dozens of species of hummingbirds with beautiful plumage and a wide array of parrots and macaws. An illusive jungle dweller is the golden Cock-of-the-Rock (*Rupicola rupicola*). The males are a golden-orange color with a crest like a Roman helmet. They have a unusual mating ritual, where the male bird clears an area of jungle floor and strikes a variety of poses while waiting for the brown-colored female to chose from among the competitors. Some males can wait for weeks and never be chosen.

HUMAN SETTLEMENTS

The most heavily populated region is the coast. About 90% of the Guyanese live and work there. The other three zones support scattered populations of mostly indigenous peoples who live off the land.

The capital city, Georgetown, has the largest urban population at about 200,000. Located at the mouth of the Demerara River, the city was founded by the British in 1781. The Dutch later claimed the settlement, but it was finally won by the British and given its present name in 1812. Georgetown is one of the best examples of a Georgian-style wooden Caribbean city. Many of the colonial buildings have been preserved as have the large tree-lined avenues built by the Dutch. Other important cities include Linden, 40 miles (64 km) south of Georgetown on the Demerara River and New Amsterdam, 50 miles (80 km) southeast of Georgetown at the mouth of the Berbice River.

All three cities are important shipment points for Guyana's most valuable mineral, bauxite. Linden and New Amsterdam are considerably smaller than Georgetown, with populations of about 60,000 and 25,000 respectively. There are many other small settlements along the coast but very few inland.

HISTORY

GUYANA HAS AN INCREDIBLY DIVERSE ethnic composition, including indigenous Amerindians and descendants of people from Africa, India, China, and Europe. This modern blend, representing all the major cultures of the world—Native American, European, Asian, and African—was not accidental, but is the result of historical events.

Guyana had two different colonial masters before independence in 1966 and much of its history has been driven by the demands of these European powers and their desire to profit from their colonies. The aftermath of colonial history continues to haunt modern Guyana through ethnic politics and discord.

Opposite: **A statue of Cuffy, who led a famous slave revolt in 1763, in Georgetown's Independence Square. Cuffy is revered as a national hero for his role in the fight for freedom.**

Left: **Supporters campaign for Guyanese independence in 1958.**

A sketch of an early Warrau village.

THE PRECOLONIAL PERIOD

Before Europeans even suspected that the Americas existed, people were already living in the area that became Guyana. These indigenous inhabitants, known today as Amerindians, were largely seminomadic, living in stable settlements for a period of time before moving their villages to new locations. They mainly practiced shifting horticulture, growing staple crops such as cassava ("kah-SAH-vah") in small farm plots, and also hunting and fishing. Most villages consisted of one or two large extended families of less than 70 people.

These villages had no formal leaders or chiefs, but important men from each of the families competed to become informal village leaders. When this competition became heated, or when the village grew too large for the farms to support the people, some members moved out to form new settlements. Each village also had a shaman, whose job included curing the sick and maintaining good relations between the people and the spirits and gods. In the Guianas (including present-day Guyana, Suriname, and French Guiana), there were several different groups of people. When the first Europeans arrived, they encountered the Karib and Arawak near the coast and the Warrau and Akawáio farther inland.

EUROPEAN DISCOVERY AND EARLY RELATIONS

Since people were already living in Guyana, it is not quite accurate to talk about "discovery" by Europeans as if they were the first inhabitants. Christopher Columbus sailed by the coast of the Guianas on his third voyage in 1498, but did not land there due to the inhospitable appearance

RALEIGH'S VISION OF GUYANA

Sir Walter Raleigh, better known for his efforts to establish a colony in Virginia, also explored what became Guyana. He made two voyages in 1595 and 1617 for Queen Elizabeth I of England, searching for the fabled El Dorado, or country of gold. This was a rumor started around the time of Columbus's early voyages that there existed a country of indigenous people whose capital city was called Manoa. Reportedly, the city and the people were covered with gold. Many adventures began in Europe with the idea of finding this legendary land, and Raleigh believed that it was inland from the Guianese coast. Although he never found Manoa or El Dorado, his writings about his travels inspired many others to seek their fortunes in the Guianas.

For example, he told the prospective explorer that he "shall find there more rich and beautiful cities, more temples adorned with golden images, than either Cortez found in Mexico, or Pizarro in Peru ...., Guiana is a country that is still untouched ...., the face of the earth is still untorn." In another passage, he described a crystal mountain covered with diamonds where waters fall. The waterfall was described as making the sound of "1,000 great bells ...., knocked one against the other." Years later, exploration of the great sandstone plateaus such as Roraima confirmed the story. Waterfalls do indeed cascade over mountains and in some light, the sand particles of the rock shine like diamonds!

of the mangrove forests and swamps along the shore. It was not until nearly a hundred years later that Dutch and English explorers and settlers began to take an interest in the Guianas. The first explorers, the most notable being Sir Walter Raleigh, brought back stories that inspired both European powers to promote colonization.

The first permanent settlement was founded in 1616 on an island in the estuary of the Essequibo River. It was led by the Dutch but included English settlers as well. This colony expanded to the Demerara River later that century and a separate Dutch colony was founded on the Berbice River. At first, Europeans settled the river banks far inland and away from the coast. The economy of these early settlements was based on growing tropical crops such as tobacco, cotton, coffee, and cocoa, and on trade with local Amerindian groups for forest products such as annatto ("ah-NAH-toh," a vegetable dye) and letter wood from trees. Unlike Spanish and Portuguese settlements elsewhere on the continent, the Dutch maintained friendly relations with the Amerindians and did not use them as slaves.

First the Dutch, and later the British, relied on the allegiance of Amerindians to help control the African slaves. Amerindians were used as militia and friendly relations were maintained with them through trade until the end of slavery in 1838.

PLANTATION SOCIETY

Throughout the latter half of the 1600s, European settlers began to move toward the coast and away from their riverine farms. At the same time, there was an economic shift from crops such as cotton and tobacco toward sugar. The first sugar plantation was started in 1658, and throughout the 1700s, the Essequibo and Demerara colonies became more and more dependent on this single crop. The Dutch set out to reclaim coastal swamp lands and protected the reclaimed land from the sea by constructing walls and dikes. Once fortified, the land was planted with large estates of sugarcane. Hundreds of thousands of Africans were imported to work on sugar and cotton plantations in the Americas, and the Dutch plantations were among the worst in terms of the abuse of human rights. The appalling conditions of slavery sparked off many minor rebellions as well as a couple of major ones in Guyana.

FIGHTING FOR CONTROL

Toward the end of the 18th century, control of the colonies at Essequibo, Demerara, and Berbice shifted several times between the British and the Dutch. The British first seized control of the three colonies in 1781. However, they only held on for a year before the French, allies of the Dutch, took back the colonies and returned them to Dutch control. In 1796 the British captured the colonies again and managed to hold on to them for six years. The Treaty of Amiens, signed in 1802, returned the colonies to the Dutch once again. This treaty held for only one year before the Netherlands and Britain once again went to war and the colonies returned to British control. All this flip-flopping ended in 1814, when the Dutch finally gave the colonies to Britain. Essequibo, Demerara, and Berbice were united in a single colony called British Guiana in 1831.

LABORING FOR SUGAR

Sugar sustained colonial Guiana and continues to be an important product in the modern economy. The wealth that it generated, however, came at the expense of many thousands of lives lost or lived in poverty and misery, first in slavery and later under the indenture system.

The life of a slave began with capture in West Africa and shipment to the New World in ships designed to hold as many people as possible. If the slave survived this horrifying journey, called "the Middle Passage," he or she would be auctioned off at one of the slave ports in South or North America. From there began a life of wretchedness. Slaves on Dutch estates were expected to work a minimum of 14 hours a day, starting at dawn. They had to work in the cane fields and do any other chores required by the estate master. In addition, they were expected to grow some of their food at night to supplement the meager rations provided by the owner. Any misbehavior was punishable by the whip and other inhumane tortures such as amputation of a leg or death by burning over a slow fire. Not surprisingly, many slaves tried to escape or revolt.

Indentured workers, primarily from India, were legally free, unlike slaves, but also suffered inhumane working and living conditions. From the point at which they signed their contracts in their home countries, their rights were ignored. Contractors often lied about conditions in Guyana to attract workers and even resorted to kidnapping unwilling workers. They, too, were crowded onto ships under unsanitary conditions and left to fend for themselves during the long journey. Some ships had mortality rates of up to 25%. Indentured workers were supposed to work a seven- or 10-hour day, depending on whether they were in the fields or the factory, but in reality often worked 11 to 18 hours a day. This was hardly any improvement over slavery.

Workers were fined for resisting the system and sometimes beaten and whipped, just as the slaves had been. They received no legal protection from the colonial state and were often arrested or killed when they "rebelled" in an attempt to get justice.

Sugar has much to answer for in the history of Guyana since it forms such a tragic part of the history of both the Afro- and Indo-Guyanese.

THE 19TH CENTURY

The most significant event in Guyana's history during the 19th century was the emancipation of African slaves that began with apprenticeship in 1834 and ended with full freedom in 1838. British Guiana was then one of the main producers of sugar in the Caribbean region. When the slaves were given their freedom, many of them decided to leave the estates and work plots of their own land. This created a severe labor shortage on the estates and plantation owners lobbied the British government to find a solution to their problem.

The solution was the indentured labor system. The indenture system works by contracting laborers in their home countries for a fixed period of work—usually five to seven years—in return for their passage to the country where they would work and either their passage home at the end

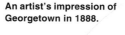

An artist's impression of Georgetown in 1888.

or the option to stay on in their new country. Wages were fixed and very low, which allowed the plantation owners to continue to produce sugar at competitive prices. Although indentured workers were formally free, the conditions of work were not that much improved from slavery.

The first group of laborers brought to Guyana under contract to work for the plantations were the English, Irish, and Germans. This trial lasted only from 1835–39 because northern Europeans were too susceptible to tropical diseases. One group, however, proved quite adaptable—the Portuguese. For 27 years, from 1835–62, a total of 31,628 Portuguese workers were brought to British Guiana. When their contracts ended, many stayed on and entered small commercial enterprises. To meet the voracious demand for labor, other countries were targeted by the indenture system—India and China.

Chinese indentured laborers began arriving in 1853. By 1912, this flow of labor was halted, but by then about 14,000 workers had come to British Guiana and many, like the Portuguese, stayed on and entered commercial trades. But by far the biggest group of workers to be imported were the East Indians. The first workers arrived in 1838 and by the time the practice was stopped due to a request from the colonial government in India in 1917, 238,960 Indians had been transported to British Guiana. They formed the backbone of plantation labor during the 19th century and went on to become the majority ethnic group in modern Guyana. At the end of their work terms, some Indians decided to return home, and 75,547 were repatriated between 1843 and 1949. Many others

A plantation worker harvests sugarcane with a machete.

stayed on at the estates, and some chose to become farmers in their new home. They developed rice agriculture in Guyana and are still the largest ethnic group in rural villages.

The indenture system helped ease the labor shortage, but sugar production never recovered after emancipation. Many small plantations could no longer compete and were bought out by bankers and other plantation owners. The result of this process was to set the stage for colonial politics in the 20th century.

BOOKER'S GUIANA

At the time of emancipation in 1838, there were 308 sugar estates. By 1904, 66 years later, there were only 46. By 1967, there were just 18, and 15 of these were controlled by a single company— Booker Brothers Company.

Emancipation meant that sugar plantation owners no longer had free labor. Although indentured labor was successfully used, it cost more, and the change from one system to the other forced many smaller plantations out of business. At the same time, people buying sugar in Britain were unhappy about having to pay more for Caribbean sugar in order to protect the plantations there. By 1836, the British government had decided to allow free competition between Caribbean planters and those in India. This also helped cause the failure and collapse of small estates. Two London-based companies that specialized in the sugar trade were Booker Brothers and John McConnell Company. Both companies benefited when the price of sugar fell in the 1880s; they were able to buy up estates that were no longer profitable.

In 1900 the two companies merged to form the Booker Brothers McConnell Company Limited. This commercial giant continued to expand ownership of ever larger estates until it controlled nearly the whole sugar industry. Booker Brothers, as it was known locally, also expanded into other parts of Guyana's economy. It owned a network of retail stores, the largest taxi service in the country, a pharmaceutical factory, and rum distilleries. It was involved in publishing, advertising, real estate, insurance, cattle ranching, and even owned its own shipping service. Until independence in 1966, Booker Brothers was the effective power in British Guiana's economy, so much so that the colony was often called "Booker's Guiana."

PREINDEPENDENCE

British Guiana entered the 20th century with an 18th century form of colonial government that had been established by the Dutch. The country was effectively controlled by estate owners rather than by the people. In 1928 Britain reformed the system, abolishing the Dutch-established councils and replacing them with a legislative council. Nevertheless, the first election for the legislative council in which everyone of adult age could vote, was not held until 1953. Meanwhile, the general population had become increasingly active in resisting British rule and British companies. The first mass political party, the People's Progressive Party (PPP), was formed in 1950 by Dr. Cheddi Jagan, an East Indian dentist, and Forbes Burnham, a black lawyer. Distinctly left-wing, the PPP won the elections of 1953, but the British governor suspended the government, claiming that this was a communist insurgence.

Forbes Burnham then broke away to form the People's National Congress (PNC). The PPP continued to win subsequent elections despite Britain's intervention, and relations in the colony continued to worsen as numerous labor strikes were violently suppressed by the authorities. Before the 1964 elections, Britain changed the voting rules so that the PPP could not win a majority. Although the PNC also failed to gain a majority, it was able to form a coalition government with the United Force (UF) that largely represented Amerindian and Portuguese interests. Secure that the left-wing PPP was shut out of power, Britain granted Guyana its freedom in 1966.

Cheddi Jagan, newly elected as prime minister, arrives in New York for informal talks with President Kennedy in 1961.

Forbes Burnham was a dominant figure in Guyanese politics for three decades until his death in 1985.

GUYANA AFTER 1966

On gaining power in the newly-independent country, Forbes Burnham set out to create a virtual dictatorship with himself and his party at the helm. In 1970 he proclaimed Guyana a cooperative republic and committed the country to a socialist economic path. In the early 1970s many foreign companies and industries were nationalized as part of this plan.

In 1980 Burnham approved a new constitution that gave the president more power. This constitution also guaranteed the right to work and affirmed the equality of women. The economy was suffering from low prices for its main exports and there were food shortages and labor unrest. Burnham cracked down on the people and was accused by local and international organizations of rigging the 1980 elections that put him in power once again. Burnham died in August 1985 and was succeeded by his vice-president, Hugh Desmond Hoyte.

Hoyte led the PNC to victory in the 1985 elections and during his term reversed some of Burnham's policies. In 1988 he began to work with the International Monetary Fund (IMF) to overhaul Guyana's economy. These changes were part of his Economic Recovery Program (ERP) designed to increase private ownership of businesses and to encourage foreign investment in Guyana. Since the 1985 elections were also questionable, Hoyte agreed to electoral reform and to have international observers, such as the Carter Center of Atlanta, present for the next round of elections. To allow enough time to make necessary changes, elections were postponed from 1990 to 1992.

Much to the dismay of the PNC, Cheddi Jagan and the PPP won the 1992 elections. Jagan set out to revise the constitution to guarantee free elections in the future. He also committed his government to Hoyte's ERP, despite the high cost being paid by Guyana's workers and poor. When Jagan died in February 1997, his vice-president, Samuel A. Hinds, became president until elections in December the same year. The PPP won the elections under their new leader, Janet Jagan, the late Cheddi Jagan's wife.

Since independence, Guyana has struggled with a failing economy and political problems. First under Burnham's dictatorship and then under the harsh economic policies of the ERP, the Guyanese have seen both their civil liberties and ability to make a living deteriorate. This has caused massive emigration to countries such as the United States, Canada, Great Britain, and other countries in the Caribbean. The economy began to turn around in 1991, but by then, many educated Guyanese had already established new homes elsewhere. Guyana is one of the poorest countries in the Western hemisphere and faces a major challenge to modernize its economy and improve human rights as it enters the next millennium.

Desmond Hoyte with Indian prime minister Rajiv Gandhi before the start of the Commonwealth Conference in Vancouver, Canada, in 1987.

GOVERNMENT

SINCE INDEPENDENCE FROM BRITISH RULE in 1966, Guyana has seen several significant changes to its constitution and to the manner in which representatives are elected to the government. Guyanese politics is largely based on party allegiance. There are five main political parties, but only two have been dominant in running the country. Guyana holds membership in many international organizations and maintains good diplomatic relations with most of the world. This chapter covers all of these issues and more.

GOVERNMENT STRUCTURE

On February 23, 1970, four years after independence from the British, Forbes Burnham, the elected prime minister at the time, turned Guyana into a cooperative republic within the Commonwealth of Nations—a group of countries that include Great Britain and its former colonies.

Opposite: **The Gothic-style city hall in George-town.**

Left: **The seat of Guyana's parliament in George-town.**

Burnham remained in power throughout the 1970s, during which time he designed a new constitution. The new constitution took effect on October 6, 1980.

Guyana's government consists of the office of the president and the elected National Assembly. The president selects a first vice-president and prime minister (both titles apply to the same person) from among the elected members of the assembly. The president is the supreme executive authority, head of state, and commander of the armed forces and is elected for a five-year term. This term can be extended by the president for periods of one year up to five times in a row so that ten years may pass between elections. There is no limit to the number of terms the same person may be president of the country.

A Guyanese man takes a break in front of a wall with electoral posters of presidential candidate Janet Jagan on the eve of elections in December 1997.

Guyana is not divided into electoral districts. The whole country is considered to be a single electing body and anyone 18 years of age with Guyanese citizenship and residing in the country on election day is eligible to vote. There are 53 elected seats in the National Assembly, and people vote for a party rather than for an individual. The party that gains the largest number of seats forms the government.

In addition, there are ten regions in Guyana, each of which has a Regional Development Council of 12 to 35 elected members. Each of these councils elects one of its members to serve in the National Assembly. Two members from each regional council also serve in the National Congress of Democratic Organs. This 20-member congress then elects two of its members to complete the available seats in the National Assembly. Thus, 53 seats are directly elected, while 12 are indirectly elected through regional councils.

SYMBOLS OF THE NATION

The flag of Guyana, which was adopted in 1966, has a green background with a white bordered yellow triangle from side to side, superimposed with a black bordered red triangle half that size. All the colors signify elements of the country and the people. Red represents the people's energy in building a new country, while black represents perseverance. Mineral wealth is represented by yellow and rivers by white. Green represents the economic resources of agriculture and forests.

The coat of arms was also adopted in 1966 and includes symbols representing people, nature, and history—an Amerindian headdress representing the original inhabitants; two diamonds representing mining; a helmet representing the monarchy (of Great Britain); a shield decorated with the national flower, the Regis water lily; two jaguars holding a pickax, sugarcane, and rice to symbolize labor and the main agricultural industries; three wavy blue lines representing Guyana's many waters; and a Canje pheasant, the national bird. The motto of the country is "One People, One Nation, One Destiny."

In addition to these elected members, non-elected Guyanese may also play important roles in government. The speaker of the house, for example, is chosen by the assembly on the first day of a new government but may not be one of the elected representatives. If the speaker is chosen from outside, he or she loses the power to cast tie-breaking votes. The president can also choose additional vice-presidents, ministers, and members of his cabinet from outside the group of elected representatives. These people become part of the government, but do not vote in the National Assembly. The president also chooses the leader of the opposition from among the elected representatives.

To vote a bill into law, one-third of the assembly must be present, and the majority must agree. The approved bill then passes to the president. If the president chooses, he or she may reject the bill and send it back to the assembly for revision. The assembly can then change the bill according to presidential instructions or, with a two-third's majority, send the bill back to the president for approval. In such a case, the president must sign the bill into law within 21 days or dissolve the assembly. In the case of dissolution, elections must be called immediately. Although the president in Guyana is powerful, he or she cannot veto a bill approved by the majority of the National Assembly.

Local government is administered by the regional councils, which are also elected for five-year terms. They can be dissolved by the president before the end of their term. Large cities such as Georgetown have elected city councils as well.

A Guyanese boy rides past an electoral banner of Desmond Hoyte, the presidential candidate of the People's National Congress, in 1997.

POLITICAL PARTIES

Guyana has more than ten registered political parties, but only two have ever formed the government. Two others have also held small numbers of seats in various governments, but have never formed the opposition. The two dominant parties are the People's Progressive Party (PPP) and the People's National Congress (PNC).

The PPP was the first party ever established in Guyana and was founded in 1950 by Dr. Cheddi Jagan. A few years later, after disagreements among party leaders, Forbes Burnham left the PPP and founded the PNC in 1955. The United Force (UF) is a small right-wing party that has generally sided with the PNC. The Working People's Alliance (WPA) began as a group promoting the rights of workers. In 1979 the group declared itself a political party. It has a left-wing, collective leadership. For the 1992 elections, Cheddi Jagan organized a coalition of left-wing opposition parties that campaigned to end electoral malpractice. This group called itself the Patriotic Coalition for Democracy (PCD) and included the PPP, WPA, Democratic Labor Movement, and the People's Democratic Movement.

THE JUDICIARY

The Supreme Court of Judicature in Guyana consists of the Court of Appeal, the High Court, and a number of Courts of Summary Jurisdiction. The High Court has jurisdiction over all civil matters referred to it by local magistrates. It has limited powers in criminal matters. Appeals are taken to either the Court of Appeal or the High Court. The chief justice is head of the High Court and is a member of the Court of Appeal.

THE MILITARY

The Guyana Defense Force (GDF) has about 7,000 members. It has its origin in the Special Service Unit (SSU) started under the British as an internal security force. Under Burnham, the SSU was converted to Guyana's army, navy, and air force, and leadership was given to black officers. In this way, the GDF was used more to contain resistance to Burnham's dictatorship than to protect Guyana's borders.

The Guyana Police Force is similarly predominantly black and was also used by Burnham to protect his position. There is also a paramilitary force called the Guyana National Service (GNS), which is made up of young people about to enter university who serve one year of national service in remote areas of the country before beginning their studies. This has been controversial, as young women traditionally do not leave home until they are married. The 1990s have seen positive changes in free elections and a shift away from PNC power. Fortunately, the military and paramilitary have not proved inflexible and have accepted these changes.

The High Court in Georgetown.

GUYANA'S FIRST WOMAN PRESIDENT

Janet Jagan was elected president of Guyana on December 15, 1997, with 54% of the vote. She replaced her deceased husband, Dr. Cheddi Jagan, as leader of the PPP. American-born, she met Dr. Jagan when he was studying dentistry in the United States in the early 1940s. They married in the United States and returned to Guyana in 1943. She has always shared his political interests. In August 1999 she announced her resignation due to ill health and named Finance Minister Bharrat Jagdeo as her successor until new elections in 2001.

FOREIGN RELATIONS

Guyana enjoys cordial relations with most other countries. Some concerns have plagued relations with neighbors, however. Both Venezuela and Suriname have, at different times, claimed land within Guyana's borders as their own. At one point, diplomatic relations with Suriname were completely severed. These were restored in 1979, but Guyana still protests

GUYANA vs. VENEZUELA

The region claimed by both Guyana and Venezuela is the eastern section of the Guiana Highlands, of which Mount Roraima is a part. This geological formation contains minerals such as bauxite, nickel, manganese, iron, diamonds, and gold, and this wealth is the reason both parties have persevered for so long. Constituting about three-fifths of Guyana's current territory, it involves land west of the Essequibo River.

The dispute started in the 19th century when the British claimed the territory for themselves. Venezuela had controlled it, but lost control when its outposts were closed due to civil war in the early 1800s. The British sent in an expedition to mark the border in 1844 and from that point on, Venezuela disputed the new international border. Venezuela asked the British to agree to abide by the decision of an international tribunal, but until the United States became involved in the 1890s, the British refused. Finally bowing to international pressure, the British agreed to the tribunal. The tribunal's decision was issued on October 3, 1899, in Paris, in an agreement since known as the Paris Tribunal, and favored the British claim. All seemed to be settled until 1944, when one of the members of the tribunal died, leaving behind a confidential document arguing that the tribunal had been biased in favor of the British. Once again, matters heated up.

When Guyana gained its independence, the new government committed itself, as did the British and the Venezuelans, to try to find a peaceful settlement. Venezuela ignored this agreement when it occupied Ankoko Island in 1968. By 1970, in order to avoid deepening the crisis, Venezuela and Guyana agreed to do nothing further for 12 years in a document known as the Port of Spain Protocol. When this period expired in 1982, the Venezuelans refused to renew it, thus opening talks once again. At this point the matter was referred to the United Nations for settlement. To date, there has been no UN proposal and the leaders of the two countries as well as the UN-appointed consultant continue to meet regularly to discuss the issue. Hoyte visited two different Venezuelan presidents in 1987 and 1989, Dr. Jagan went in 1993, and Janet Jagan paid a visit to President Rafael Caldera in July 1998. Relations have improved considerably since the tense 1960s, but neither side has conceded its claim.

that Surinamese maps include a part of its territory in the southeast. The dispute with Venezuela goes back to colonial times. Although neither party has agreed to let the matter drop, conflict has been confined to the diplomatic level. Guyana is a member of the Treaty for Amazon Cooperation signed in 1978 with Brazil, Bolivia, Colombia, Ecuador, Peru, Suriname, and Venezuela. Guyana is also a member of the Commonwealth of Nations, the Economic Commission for Latin America and the Caribbean, the Food and Agriculture Organization, the Inter-American Development Bank, and the Association of Caribbean States.

ECONOMY

GUYANA FACES UNIQUE ECONOMIC PROBLEMS and challenges due to its small size, its limited resources, and its colonial heritage. Since independence, the various governments have tried two radically different strategies to improve the standard of living for the Guyanese. Both have resulted in impoverishment for different reasons. While the future looks brighter now than it has for many years, the people continue to struggle to make ends meet in this very poor country.

TWO PATHS TO DEVELOPMENT

From 1970 on, Burnham instituted a number of major economic reforms, changing the British system. He renamed Guyana a cooperative republic. His goal was to create a socialist economy in which major industries were owned and run on a cooperative basis. This meant that there could be no foreign ownership, so Burnham set out to nationalize the country's main

Opposite: **A bauxite plant and metal scrap pile in Linden.**

Left: **A man nets shrimp in an irrigation canal near the coast.**

foreign-controlled companies. The biggest were the Booker Brothers' sugar interests, the Demerara Bauxite Company (owned by Canada's ALCAN), and American-owned Reynolds Mines (also a bauxite mining interest). Besides sugar and bauxite, Burnham also created a number of government-owned enterprises to produce or manage every other aspect of the economy and nationalized 29 other companies.

By 1975, Guyana was in economic difficulty when the prices for both bauxite and sugar declined on the world market. Burnham borrowed money to keep the economy going, but this only increased Guyana's foreign debt. Inflation ballooned, and by 1989, four years after Burnham's death, Guyana had replaced Haiti as the poorest country in the Western hemisphere.

After coming into office as Burnham's successor, Desmond Hoyte began to negotiate with international agencies such as the International Monetary Fund (IMF) to restructure the economy and to renegotiate the debt. In 1987 Hoyte introduced the Economic Recovery Program (ERP), which reversed the policies of Burnham. Under the ERP, Guyana began to encourage foreign investment and sold some government companies to private owners. For example, a new bauxite mine was opened in

ALL THAT IS GOLD DOES NOT GLITTER

The Omai Gold Mine began production in 1993 on the Omai River, a tributary of the Essequibo. It is jointly owned by a Canadian company, an American company, and the Guyanese government. The deposit was believed to hold an estimated 3.6 million ounces (135,000 kg) of gold, and the plan was to mine it over 10 years. The mine is an open-pit mine, in which large holes are dug in the earth to get at the rocks containing gold. Once the rocks are crushed, a process called cyanide leaching separates out the gold. As the name implies, cyanide, a highly toxic poison, is the main chemical used in this process. It evaporates quickly, but long-term exposure to even low levels of cyanide can cause mental retardation.

In August 1995 disaster struck when a waste pond collapsed, leaking 4.2 million cubic yards (3.2 million cubic meters) of cyanide-contaminated waste into the river. People reported seeing fish and animals floating dead in the river far downstream. The Omai Mine was closed for six months while American and Canadian experts conducted an investigation. Although the American firm had been involved in other incidences due to poor quality equipment and construction, no action was taken against these companies. They agreed to pay US$10 million in damages and resumed production in 1996 with no modifications to their mining practices.

Aroima with Reynolds and a gold mine concession on the Omai River was granted to foreign companies. Sugarcane land was not sold back to Booker, but Booker Tate, the successor to Booker Brothers McConnell, was hired to oversee sugar production in order to boost output.

One of the demands of the IMF was that the government had to reduce expenses. As a result, many government workers lost their jobs. In one bauxite mine alone, 700 of its 3,000 workers were laid off between 1992 and 1994, with plans to let another 1,100 go in the future. Guyana was also forced to allow its currency, the Guyana dollar, to "float," that is, let it reflect the true strength of the Guyanese economy on the world market. Effectively a devaluation of the currency, more and more dollars were thus needed to buy the same amount of foreign goods. Called "structural adjustment," many of the world's poorer and indebted nations have had to go through these changes. But while it improves production, exports, and the government's ability to pay its debts, it does not improve the lives of the people. The Guyanese saw their standard of living plummet, the result of high unemployment and inflation. This prompted massive emigration in the late 1980s and early 1990s.

Opposite: **Vendors at a street market in Georgetown.**

MAIN INDUSTRIES

A worker hauls rice in a mill near Georgetown. The cultivation of rice depends on careful irrigation, so the farmers are dependent on the smooth functioning of the dams and dikes that control water flow along the coast. Guyanese rice is long-grained and highly sought after in European countries such as the Netherlands.

AGRICULTURE Agriculture is the biggest sector of the economy. The narrow coastal zone supports the two main export crops, sugar and rice, which together account for about 45% of all exports. Sugar is still produced on large estates using manual labor. Because of the clay-based soil, machines cannot easily be used in Guyana. Instead, the fields must be fertilized, planted, and cut by hand. This is grueling work in the hot sun and employs up to 24,000 workers in peak season. As sugarcane is a seasonal produce, not all of these people have work all year long.

Rice is the second most important agricultural product. Unlike sugar, it is grown on relatively small family plots. East Indian laborers began to grow rice when they finished their labor contracts in the 19th and 20th centuries. Today, they still make up the majority of rice farmers, who number about 24,000. Other agricultural crops include coconuts, oranges, bananas, and plantains. Much of the land in the savannas is used for cattle ranching, since it is not fertile enough for agriculture.

FORESTRY AND FISHING Tropical rainforest covers about three-quarters of Guyana but until the 1990s was underexploited, although there has always been some harvesting of trees, especially valuable hardwoods. In 1991 the government gave out the largest timber concession ever to a foreign company to produce plywood in a Georgetown factory. Plywood exports to the United States quadrupled as a result of this deal. Shrimp fishing in the ocean is the main focus of the commercial fishing industry. American and Japanese companies control much of this industry.

MINING Bauxite and gold together represent some 38% of Guyana's exports. Bauxite mining started in Guyana in 1916, with the biggest mine in Linden and a second mine in the Berbice River region. Bauxite can be processed to produce calcium carbonate and alumina, which is the key constituent in aluminum. Although bauxite is a valuable export, it does

An aerial view of a lumber mill along a river.

A sugar factory in west Demerara. When it is time to harvest, the sugarcane fields are burned to remove the leaves from the cane and to clear out cane rats and snakes. Then the cane is cut with machetes and bundled together. The bundles are carried to nearby canals, where they are floated in small boats to the processing plants.

not require large numbers of workers, since machines can do much of the work. It is also subject to large price fluctuations, which makes the exporting country vulnerable to economic ups and downs. In addition, more and more developed countries are now recycling aluminum, thus reducing demand and pushing down prices. Nevertheless, with the new mine in Aroima, Guyana will continue to mine bauxite and be dependent on the money it brings to the economy. Gold has been mined on a small scale for many years, but only in 1993 did the government grant a large concession to a foreign firm. Since then, gold revenues have grown and make a significant contribution to export earnings, though the mine does not employ a large number of people.

MANUFACTURING As well as growing and extracting raw materials, Guyana also processes these materials and produces manufactured goods, such as clothing, rum, and food. This is a small sector of the economy, accounting for only 11% of the value of domestic production.

THE WORKFORCE

Guyana's labor force totals about 270,000 people, including 80,000 women. Agriculture, forestry, and fishing employ about 48,500; mining employs 9,500; manufacturing represents 28,000 workers; construction and trade take 23,800; 2,900 people work in financial services; transportation and communications employ 9,200; while the service industry is the largest employer with 57,500.

About 50,000 are unemployed and the rest are engaged in activities not clearly defined. Two trends are evident in employment—the rising unemployment over the last 20 years and the growing number of women in the labor force. Both trends reflect the weak economy and the effects of the Economic Recovery Program inaugurated in 1987, which has forced more people out of work and out to look for work.

CARICOM AND FREE TRADE

In 1967 Guyana became one of the signatories to the Caribbean Free Trade Area, which later became the Caribbean Community and Common Market (CARICOM) in 1973. Members of CARICOM include all the former British colonies in the Caribbean Basin. The Secretariat of CARICOM is located in Georgetown. In 1991 CARICOM signed a trade cooperation agreement with the United States, the first step for the Caribbean countries to become part of the American plan to unite the whole Western hemisphere in a single trade agreement.

This would eventually mean that all products produced anywhere in North, Central, or South America, or the Caribbean would be available to consumers in the entire region with no extra taxes. Currently, many countries protect their producers with special taxes on imports. Smaller economies such as Guyana's are concerned about competing with giants such as the United States and Canada, but free trade would give all the Americas an advantage in competition with other trading blocs such as the European Union. CARICOM is the first step along this path for Guyana.

TRADE

Guyana's main trading partners for exports are the European Union,
Canada, the United States, CARICOM countries, and Japan. Its chief
imports are fuel and lubricants, heavy equipment, and manufactured
consumer goods such as appliances. Guyana mainly imports from
CARICOM countries, the United States, the European Union, Japan, and
Canada (in descending value of imports).

TRANSPORTATION

In the coastal zone, there are more than 3,000 miles (4,830 km) of paved
and good-weather roads linking towns and villages. However, outside this
zone, there are virtually no highways. A road linking Linden and
Georgetown was upgraded in 1993. Work on a second highway linking
Georgetown with Lethem, on the Brazilian border, was begun in 1989, but
is still only about half completed due to a lack of funds. There are no

public railways in the country, although two small private lines operate to transport minerals from the mines to the ports. Most people living in the interior of the country are either completely isolated from the coast or travel by air to make the journey over dense forests. Depending on the point of origin and the destination, river travel is also common, as there are some 607 miles (977 km) of navigable rivers.

Guyana has a government-owned airline called Guyana Airways Corporation. It links the major settlements in the interior with the coast and has regular flights to destinations such as Canada and the United States leaving from Timehri International Airport, 26 miles (42 km) from Georgetown. Guyana has two seaports. The older is in Georgetown and was built to handle the transportation of sugar. The second is in New Amsterdam and was constructed primarily to ship bauxite and its derivatives.

A water taxi in Parika along the Essequibo River.

THE GUYANESE

GUYANA HAS A POPULATION of 707,954 (1998 estimate). One of the many names for Guyana is "Land of Six Peoples." This refers to the main ethnic groups that form the majority of the country's population—East Indian, African, Chinese, Portuguese, British, and Amerindian. All but one of these groups—the exception being the Amerindians—came to or were brought to Guyana because of sugar. As a result of the specific history of their arrival, different groups have come to occupy different niches in society.

ETHNIC GROUPS

Although the popular conception of Guyana is that it is composed of six groups—East Indian, African, Chinese, Portuguese, British, and

Opposite: **Elementary schoolgirls in George-town.**

Left: **Residents of the town of Bartica.**

49

THE GUYANESE

The Afro-Guyanese tend to live in towns, especially Georgetown. When slaves were finally freed in the 19th century, they chose to distance themselves from plantation society as quickly as possible. Many of them moved to urban areas and began to educate themselves to occupy better paying positions in the economy. From there, they expanded into the civil service and the bauxite industry. Today, the Afro-Guyanese make up about 50% of the urban population.

Amerindian—the actual breakdown of the population is rather more complex, with a seventh important group, those with mixed African and European ancestry, included. Breakdown of the population by ethnicity cannot be precise in part because people sometimes identify themselves differently at different times and because census categories have changed over time. Based on the most recent estimates and figures available, the following percentages can be identified:

- Indo-Guyanese (people descended from East Indian immigrants): 49%
- Afro-Guyanese (people descended from African slaves and immigrants): 32%
- Mixed (people descended from African and European unions): 12%
- Amerindians (indigenous groups): 6%
- Portuguese and other Europeans: 0.5%
- Chinese: 0.5%

The mixed group includes people with both African and European ancestors. Under slavery, it was not uncommon for a white master to have relations with his female slaves. Later, when indentured laborers arrived without wives of their own, they sometimes married women of African origin. The percentages above make clear that the two biggest groups are those of East Indian and African descent.

Portuguese and Chinese are also included in the "six" races, although their numbers are quite small. Whites, or those of European descent, are also a tiny minority. Amerindians represent a larger percentage of the population. Guyana is one of the few countries in the Americas where the number of original peoples has held steady or even increased in the 20th century.

Not only is the population as a whole complexly divided by ethnicity, but even within these larger categories there are differences and specificities.

INDO-GUYANESE People of East Indian descent make up the largest ethnic group. They can be divided into two subgroups—those who practice Hinduism and those who practice Islam as their religion. Unlike in India, where these differences have led to war and the separation of Pakistan and Bangladesh from India, the two subgroups of Indo-Guyanese live amicably in Guyana.

AFRO-GUYANESE AND MIXED The descendants of African slaves and the mixture of these people with Europeans constitute what is called Creole society. Although the slaves came from many different cultural groups in West Africa, they have lost most of the cultural and linguistic characteristics that separated them. This is a very common process wherever slaves were brought to live and is the result of the conditions of slavery in which the slaves were not allowed to maintain cultural differences among themselves. The main differences among the Afro-Guyanese are those of color, with the mixed group traditionally occupying a slightly higher position in society.

Indo-Guyanese vendors in Parika. Generally, the Indo-Guyanese tend to live in rural areas. When East Indian laborers completed their work contracts, they tended to either continue to work for the sugar plantations or, if they had enough money, they bought land and began to plant rice. Today, the Indo-Guyanese represent about 80% of the rural population.

AMERINDIANS The Amerindian group is not uniform, but is made up of people from a number of smaller linguistic and cultural groups. Three indigenous languages are represented among Guyana's Amerindians— Karib, Arawak, and Warrau.

Among the Karib-speaking groups found in modern Guyana are the Akawáio, Patamuno (a subtribe of the Akawáio), Arekuna, Parukoto and Taulipáng (both subgroups of the Arekuna), Ingarikó, and Makushí. The Akawáio live near the Guyana-Venezuela-Brazil border and continue to practice traditional ways. The Patamuno live in the Pakaraima Mountains between the Ireng River and the Kaieteur escarpment. They have mostly integrated into the Guyanese cash economy.

Amerindian women in Orinduik, near the border with Brazil.

GUYANA'S PREHISTORY

Before the arrival of Europeans, most indigenous groups in the Amazon Basin and surrounding region relied on small-scale farming, hunting, and fishing. For this reason, they are usually classified first by language family rather than by distinct economic practices. Karib refers to a family of related languages rather than to one single language. Karib-speaking peoples are thought to have come from an area in the Amazon River valley now in modern Brazil. They began to migrate northward around A.D. 1200, and by 1300 they were expanding into the Lesser Antilles (part of the islands of the Caribbean). There, they intermarried with members of another language family, the Arawak. In this process, Karib was lost, so that by the time Europeans encountered indigenous people on the islands, they spoke only Arawak languages. Karib speakers remained on the mainland in northern Venezuela, the Guianas, and parts of Brazil. Arawak speakers also inhabited parts of the mainland and were trying to expand along the northern coast of South America before European settlement. The third language group is Warrau. People of this group are found today between the Orinoco River in Venezuela and the Pomeroon River in Guyana. This is a swampy region, and it has been postulated that they moved here to escape the warlike Karib and Arawak speakers as the latter two groups expanded their territories.

The Arekuna arrived in Guyana in the 1920s when Seventh Day Adventist missionaries were expelled from Venezuela. They followed the missionaries and still live in the Paruima area of Guyana. The Parukoto live on both sides of the border with Venezuela and have experienced population growth in the 20th century due to missionary work and the introduction of Western medicine. Their lifestyle is now threatened by miners coming into the region looking for gems.

The Taulipáng live near Roraima. This group was almost decimated by the mass immigration of Brazilians into their territory in the mid-19th century. They are still aware of their tribal heritage, but increasingly they speak Portuguese and Spanish as their first languages. The Makushí live in the savanna region of Rupununi and in the southern Pakaraimas of Guyana and Venezuela. They are a large group who have adapted to Guyanese values and technology. In Rupununi, many are cattle ranchers.

The two Arawak-speaking groups are the Locono and Taruma. The Locono live along the coast from the Moruka River in Guyana to the Brazil-French Guiana border. Their population is growing and they have integrated into the coastal economy of the region.

The Ingarikó live near the Guyana-Brazil border on the Mau River. They have had some contact with Brazilian society, but have also managed to maintain their traditional language and culture.

The story of the Taruma is tragic. They migrated into the southern part of Guyana in the 18th century and were about 500 strong in the 19th century. In the 1920s an epidemic of influenza almost wiped out the Taruma. Today, there are a few descendants of this group who still refer to themselves as Taruma. Unfortunately, such stories are common as indigenous peoples with no natural immunity to many European diseases fall sick. These diseases have been introduced to the Amazon by miners and explorers and spread very rapidly. It is thus remarkable that Guyana's population of indigenous people is now growing.

The third group are the Warrau, who live in the lowland delta of the Orinoco River in Venezuela. Unlike forest dwellers, these people are mostly dependent on fishing and are proficient boat-builders.

Amerindian sisters in the settlement of Cabacaburi.

PORTUGUESE The Portuguese indentured laborers were mostly drawn from a single island off the coast of Portugal—Madeira. This is one of the islands of the Azores group, and due to poverty and a tradition of emigration, Madeira has supplied many labor needs around the world from the 19th century to the present.

CHINESE The Chinese workers were largely drawn from the south of China and therefore spoke Cantonese rather than the northern and dominant Chinese language, Mandarin. Much like Madeira, the region of Canton, now called Guangdong, has traditionally been poorer than the north and was a major exporter of workers to many parts of the world throughout the 19th and early 20th centuries.

POPULATION PATTERNS

Guyana has an unusual demographic pattern. On the one hand, because 90% of the people live in a small area along the coast, Guyana appears to be overpopulated and experiences the problems that accompany that condition—urban crime and inadequate public services. On the other hand, given the actual size of the country, the population density is only about 8.5 people per square mile (3.3 people per square km). That means Guyana is underpopulated and experiences associated problems, such as a failure to fully exploit its natural resources for lack of labor.

Growth-wise, Guyana experienced a fairly constant growth pattern throughout most of the 20th century. The population reached a peak of over one million in the late 1980s. A significant factor in this growth was the introduction of DDT in the 1940s to combat malaria.

Since the late 1980s, there has been a dramatic decline in Guyana's population to about 700,000 in the late 1990s. The economic repercussions of the ERP encouraged emigration. As the economy worsened, more and more people decided to leave and find a better life in the more developed countries to the north, especially Canada and the United States. Unfortunately for Guyana, most of those who left were the better-educated Guyanese.

Guyanese line up to cast their votes in the December 1997 elections. In the 1950s there was hope that the two main groups, the Indo- and Afro-Guyanese, would unite politically, since the original PPP was founded by representatives from both sides. However, Forbes Burnham succumbed to pressure from the British colonial office to form a separate party and took most of the Afro-Guyanese support with him. Since then, the split has remained at the political level.

ETHNIC TENSIONS

The main ethnic tension exists between the two largest groups, the Indo-Guyanese and Afro-Guyanese. The Afro-Guyanese are generally considered by others—and consider themselves—to be almost native to the country, while the Indo-Guyanese are usually grouped with the Portuguese and the Chinese as "immigrants." These two groups have competed since independence for dominance in politics, with the PPP representing people of East Indian descent and the PNC being largely supported by the Afro-Guyanese.

This ethnic tension is unfortunate but perhaps not surprising given the history of relations between the two groups under colonialism. The British used ethnic and racial differences to prevent groups of workers from uniting against the exploitative planter class. Under extreme economic pressure, ethnic tensions can escalate. If the new government can continue to lead the country out of trouble, there will be another chance for the main groups to work together for a common future.

CUFFY

In 1763 one of the most successful slave rebellions of the century took place in Berbice colony, then under Dutch control. The rebellion started in February that year on the Magdalenenburg plantation and quickly spread to other plantations in the area. By the end of March, almost the whole colony was under slave control and their leaders swore that they would never return to a life of servility and cruelty. One of these slave leaders was Cuffy. Cuffy and the other slaves managed to hold the colony for ten months despite the Dutch efforts to reclaim it. With the help of Amerindians and soldiers from the Netherlands, the colony was finally retaken by the end of the year and the rebel leaders rounded up and executed. Cuffy is regarded as a hero in Guyana for his part in this rebellion, and there is a statue of him in Georgetown.

SOME FAMOUS GUYANESE

REVEREND JOHN SMITH Reverend John Smith was a member of the London Missionary Society who came to work in Guyana in the early 19th century. He campaigned against the atrocities committed by the planters against their slaves. After a slave uprising in Demerara colony in 1823, he was falsely accused of having helped the slaves to rebel. He was imprisoned and died in prison. His death added fuel to the abolitionist movement—the movement to end slavery—in Britain.

WALTER RODNEY On June 23, 1980, Walter Rodney was given a people's funeral in Guyana. He was a historian who graduated from the University of the West Indies and later received his doctorate from the University of London. He wrote about the history of European exploitation and imperialism in the Caribbean and in his own country. He was also a founding member of the Working People's Alliance Party (WPA), and this earned him the animosity of the dictatorial government of Forbes Burnham.

Government forces were widely believed to have been involved in his assassination. Despite a government directive that no civil servants should attend his funeral, thousands of people accompanied his body on the day of the funeral. He joins other great Afro-Caribbean writers who have analyzed the role of Europe in creating poverty in the Americas. He became a symbol of the oppression of the Burnham government.

Laurens Storm Van's Gravesande was the Dutch governor of the colony of Essequibo from 1742–72. In 1746 he opened up the Demerara region for colonization and encouraged many Dutch and British planters to move from their estates in the Caribbean islands. He is remembered for his work as governor and also for his support for humane treatment of slaves on the plantations.

LIFESTYLE

WITH SUCH A DIVERSE ETHNIC MIX, it is impossible to generalize about the lifestyle of the Guyanese people. The most important differences are those between rural and urban dwellers and between Indo- and Afro-Guyanese cultures. Some social institutions are shared by all the Guyanese, such as education and health, but even in these areas, there are some differences. In this chapter, we will consider such issues as family structure, social interaction, and literacy.

FAMILY STRUCTURE

There are three main patterns of family life in Guyana and they correspond roughly to ethnic and class groupings. Due to different conditions of life under the colonial system, the Afro-, Indo-, and Euro-Guyanese developed different types of family structures or modified those that they brought with them from their country of origin.

Opposite: **A mother and daughter in Georgetown.**

Left: **A horse cart hauls rice through a street in Georgetown.**

A woman merchant selling groceries at Bourda Market in Georgetown. More and more women are entering the labor force to add to the family income.

AFRO-GUYANESE As slaves, Africans were not encouraged or allowed to maintain their original kinship and family ties, and much of the African culture they came with died out quickly on the plantations. In its place European models were introduced. The Afro-Guyanese are part of what became known as Creole culture, the result of copying European models with modifications due to poverty and economic conditions.

Today, Afro-Guyanese family structure has two facets—the reality and the ideal. In the ideal family, young people marry at a formal wedding and then set up house together where the man works and his wife stays home. The reality for the majority of Creoles or Afro-Guyanese is radically different. Because men have not been able to guarantee financial support for their girlfriends, women have chosen to not marry and instead raise their children (often by several different men) in their natal homes, with their mothers, grandmothers, and sisters to help. Women become the main support of the family, and the men move in and out of this unit as and when they are able to provide some support. This matrifocal or mother-centered pattern is common across the Caribbean.

MARRIAGE HINDU-STYLE IN GUYANA

After the prospective bride and groom have convinced their parents of their choice of partner, the young people step aside and the older generation takes over. There are many steps that have to be followed for the wedding to conform to the rules of the Hindu religion and the local traditions of the family or village. Some of the events that make up a wedding in Guyana include:

Chekai ("che-KAI") or engagement ceremony: The bride's father offers gifts to the groom's father and a religious scholar known as a *pandit* ("PAHN-dit") invokes the blessings of Hindu gods and goddesses. Other male members of the community are present to show that they approve of the marriage.

Tilak ("TEE-lahk"): Another ceremony that takes place at the groom's house. The *pandit* will ask the groom to behave himself and dedicate his life to his bride.

Hardi ("HAHR-dee"): The bride and groom are purified by *pandits*, and neighbors bring small gifts to each house.

Kumari-patra ("koo-MAHR-ee PAH-trah") and *kumar-patra* ("koo-MAHR PAH-trah"): Ceremonies held to mark the end of childhood for both bride and groom.

INDO-GUYANESE Both the ideal and reality are also quite different among the Guyanese of East Indian descent. As indentured laborers, East Indians were encouraged to maintain their culture and not mix with either the former slaves or other indentured groups. At the end of their contract, they were encouraged to stay in the colony with grants of small plots of land near the sugar estates. This kept them available for paid work on the plantations and avoided payment of their passage home—an obligatory part of the indenture contract. As more and more East Indians settled in the rural areas, they brought their wives over and tried to recreate their traditional family structure. They managed to keep some of their traditions alive, but some were not sustainable because of their small numbers.

One cultural trait that was not maintained was the caste system. This is a social hierarchy in which people are considered more or less religiously pure, according to the traditional job held by members of the family. All families doing the same work were considered to be of the same caste. In India, people generally do not marry outside of their caste, and the rules are very strict. In Guyana, East Indians could not continue this custom because there just were not enough people from each caste to provide a suitable range of marriageable partners.

Nevertheless, other features of Indian social life were maintained, including religion and a strong family life. Today, the Indo-Guyanese place a great deal of emphasis on marriage, children, and maintaining ties with the extended family. Marriages are no longer arranged by the parents as young people assert their rights to choose their partners. However, both sets of parents are involved in preparing for the wedding and helping the young couple to get started in life.

Since the Indo-Guyanese can be either Muslim or Hindu, they used to marry only within their religion. That is still the ideal and the norm, but marriages across religious lines are possible, if not encouraged. What is not allowed is marriage into other ethnic groups, particularly Creole society. In this way, culture has been preserved from one generation to the next. Hindu weddings are common colorful events on the weekends in rural areas during the dry season.

Young Indo-Guyanese women shopping in Georgetown's Stabroek Market.

EURO-GUYANESE The third cultural pattern is that set by European immigrants. Here, as in other colonies, the Europeans were the wealthiest and could afford elaborate weddings and stable marriages. Their ideal was to marry only people of high rank and white ethnic background. Family ties are important because this group is so small today that they must rely on one another for help.

RURAL VS. URBAN LIVING The majority of the Indo-Guyanese live in small rural villages along the coast. Here, traditional rites and festivities are maintained more strictly and family ties are broadened with each generation's marriages. A marriage here means not just the union of two young people, but also of their families. This is the basis for social cohesion.

In urban centers, marriage is still important and still involves the two families, but may not be as significant in terms of economic cooperation and the inheritance of land and other forms of wealth. Creole people live

Women board a boat at Bartica.

in both cities and villages, but are more urban than rural. In general, urban families are smaller due to the constraints of housing. At the same time, there are more families that include the father, since men are more likely to find work and be able to live near both their families and their jobs.

Rural families are often poorer, but live in better conditions than the poor of the cities, who must contend with unsanitary conditions and higher crime rates. Crime is more prevalent in the cities because people can hide in crowds and because the concentration of people attracts those who wish to live by illegal means. In the countryside, people know one another so it is not so easy to get away with crimes against your neighbors. The benefits of city living are easier access to education and other services and greater potential for paid employment for those who do not have land in the countryside.

A street in Bartica.

HOUSING

Housing styles reflect wealth and local conditions. Traditional building patterns on the coast have left a heritage of beautiful, raised wooden houses in cities such as Georgetown. Farther inland, houses take on different shapes, depending on their location, from the more ranch-like designs in the savanna to conical, thatched Amerindian houses in the more isolated settlements.

EDUCATION AND LITERACY

Guyanese children must attend school between the ages of 6 and 14 years. Elementary education covers the first six years, while secondary education begins at age 12 and lasts for five to seven years, divided into two cycles of five and two years. Enrollment figures for elementary and secondary education are 82% and 57% of the school-age population respectively. Guyana boasts a very high literacy rate of 95% for people over the age of 15.

An Amerindian home in the interior.

SHIRT-JACS FOR THE MODERN GUYANESE

Formal dress for men in Guyana used to require a long-sleeved cuffed shirt and trousers. In the intense heat and humidity of the tropics, this was not a comfortable option. Since independence, political leaders have been popularizing a type of shirt called a shirt-jac. This is buttoned up but not tucked in and has at least three pockets on the front. It is white or some other light color and made of light fabrics such as cotton. The pockets can be decorated with pleats, but otherwise the shirt is unadorned. It is also open in a "V" at the top with lapels. A more practical formal dress, the shirt-jac has become quite popular with Guyanese men.

Despite this impressive level of basic literacy skills, the school system has suffered from severe under funding, as well as staffing and supply problems for many years. Schools from kindergarten to university have all been provided by the government since Burnham made them public in 1976. This allows universal access, as everyone, no matter how poor, can enroll in a public school. This has done much to boost literacy. During the economic crisis of the 1980s, however, the quality of education suffered tremendously. Guyanese high school students must take an examination set by the University of London in England to graduate. Called the General Certificate of Education, student scores have plummeted in the last decade. There are several reasons for this deterioration.

Schoolchildren in Bartica.

AN ALTERNATIVE LIFESTYLE: PORK-KNOCKERS

Pork-knockers are a rare breed of men who spend their lives in Guyana's interior, sifting through river mud looking for rough diamonds and gold nuggets. Pork-knockers used to be mostly Afro-Guyanese, but in recent years, with the failing economy, young Indo-Guyanese are trying their hand, too. The gold-miners use pumps to dredge the silt from the bottom of the river into pans with mesh at the bottom. The silt is then separated from larger pebbles and rocks, some of which contain gold. The miners then melt the gold nuggets together and when they have enough, make their way into the nearest settlement to sell their hard-earned riches.

Diamond hunters dig holes along the river banks and sort through the mud and rocks looking for gems. Guyana's diamonds are small but of high quality. The largest ever found, in 1970, was eight karats, but it mysteriously disappeared. The three men who found that diamond are still pork-knockers and as poor as ever. Although the pork-knockers are constantly finding gold and diamonds, they never get rich, because when they sell their treasures, they spend all their money immediately, eating, drinking, and living well after weeks in the jungle. This is much the same pattern as what happened during the Gold Rush in the United States in the 19th century. It's a different way of life and definitely not for everyone!

The main problem is that the government does not have the money to fund a completely free system. School buildings cannot be properly maintained, and there are shortages of texts and teaching materials. Under the PNC dictatorship, schools were also used to promote party politics and loyalty. Teachers who did not agree were fired, leaving fewer qualified teachers and an atmosphere of insecurity in the teaching profession. Since the ERP was implemented to repair the economy, Guyana has lost many of its professionals, including teachers, to emigration. All of these factors contributed to creating a poor learning environment.

Beyond secondary school, there are several technical and vocational institutes and three teacher training colleges, as well as a national university. The University of Guyana was set up after independence. It is free to Guyanese citizens and offers undergraduate degrees in the arts and sciences. However, in order to enter classes, every student has to join the National Service for one year, during which they perform development work in remote areas. National Service was also another way the government used education to indoctrinate young people about politics. The new government has included educational reform as part of what it hopes to accomplish during its term of office.

HEALTH

Medical services remain inadequate in Guyana. There are 30 hospitals, supplemented by 162 health centers in the country, and a ratio of one doctor for every 6,200 people. The main public hospital in Georgetown, Georgetown Public Hospital, is understaffed, overcrowded, and suffers from inadequate supplies of medicines. There are also private hospitals, but they too lack medicines. Medicine is imported and requires foreign currency, a luxury neither the government nor the people of Guyana can afford in the current economic situation. As a result, some of the Guyanese have turned to an alternative healing practice called Kali Mai Puja ("KAH-lee MAI POO-jah").

To compound the problem, Guyana is a tropical country that is vulnerable to many of the most infectious and deadly diseases known to humankind. Dengue fever is on the rise and typhoid is present. Gastroenteritis, a disease of the stomach and intestine, is common as are intestinal parasites. One intestinal parasite found in Guyana is microfilaria, which if left untreated, causes noninfectious elephantiasis, the extreme growth of parts of the body to the point where they cannot be structurally supported. Malaria is no longer a problem along the coast, but is

KALI MAI: DESTRUCTION OF EVIL FORCES

There is a small group of people who believe in the powers of a specific ritual to cure sick people, particularly those with emotional and psychological problems. The ritual is called Kali Mai Puja. *Puja* is an East Indian word for a religious ritual that shows devotion to one of the Hindu gods or goddesses. In this particular ritual, the goddess Kali is prayed to for help. Kali is believed to be the goddess of destruction, but she can also destroy evil. A Kali Mai Puja requires a specialist to preside over activities called a *pujari* ("POO-jah-ree").

This person can be of either gender and can come from any cultural background. Followers of Kali Mai say that the rituals are drawn from all the religions in Guyana and therefore can work for anyone. Kali Mai works through possession by spirits and animal sacrifice. There is even a Kali Mai Church and the only requirement for membership is that the person reject their former religious beliefs. Some psychologists have used Kali Mai *pujaris* to help with their patients' problems. Although not widely popular, it is a distinctly Guyanese religion and alternative healing practice.

still very common inland and is on the rise. Malaria is passed on by the anopheles mosquito when it bites humans. Certain kinds of malaria are fatal. Yellow fever is also present, and many types of skin fungal infections are endemic due to the high humidity and lack of medical treatment. Tuberculosis has plagued the population for a long time, and the government has sponsored several antituberculosis campaigns. This disease is highly contagious and difficult to control. There are also occasional hepatitis epidemics in populated areas.

Many of these diseases, especially in coastal areas, result from inadequate supplies of water and inadequate public hygiene. Most rainwater and wash water are collected in open drains in the cities and towns. In richer neighborhoods, sewage is disposed of using septic tanks, but in the poorer areas, it is allowed to run off in open drains. Similarly, garbage is allowed to pile up in public places in poorer areas. Stagnant water and garbage encourage the spread of diseases such as typhoid, dengue, gastroenteritis, and parasitic infections. Public water supplies are also unsafe in both rural and urban areas.

As with education, the new government has promised to improve health services, but this will only be possible if Guyana can boost its economy so that it can afford expensive imports or qualify for international loans to upgrade its overworked healthcare sector.

Opposite: **A young Amerindian with a broken arm boards a boat to take him to a hospital ten hours away.**

RELIGION

AS WITH ETHNICITY, diversity is the key to religion in Guyana. Almost all the world's main religions have some representation here, along with minor cults and folk belief systems. Religion has also played an important role in historical and modern-day political relations among the various groups.

THE MAIN FORMAL RELIGIONS

Current statistics suggest that 57% of Guyanese are Christian, the majority of whom are Anglican and come from the British and Creole ethnic groups. The Portuguese are Roman Catholic. Hindus represent 33% of the population and are all of East Indian descent. Muslims make up 9%, and while most are East Indian, there are a few Afro-Guyanese Muslims as well.

Opposite: **St. George's Anglican Cathedral in Georgetown dates from 1889.**

Left: **A spiritual university in Georgetown.**

A father and daughter in their best Sunday clothes going to church.

CHRISTIANS The Anglican Church is the official church of England and the religion was brought to Guyana by British planters during the colonial period. The Anglican Church is similar to the Roman Catholic Church in many ways, but Anglicans do not regard the Pope as the head of the church. The English monarch (currently Queen Elizabeth II) is considered to be the "defender of the faith." While Anglicans also hold Mass, like Roman Catholics, they are allowed to divorce, which is forbidden in the Roman Catholic Church. Most Creoles adopted this religion while they were slaves and continue to practice it today. Since all education in Guyana was controlled by church groups until 1956, there was some pressure for East Indian children to convert while they attended school. Some did so, but the majority have held on to Hinduism and Islam, their religions of birth.

HINDUS Hinduism is the dominant religion in India. It is a pantheistic religion, meaning that there are many different deities or gods. Since 1875, there have been two sects of Hinduism—Sanatan Dharam or the Orthodox sect, and Arya Samaj or the Reformist sect. Followers of Sanatan Dharam believe in the most traditional of Hindu writings and practices. They worship all the traditional gods and goddesses, such as Ganesh, Lakshmi, and Agni, and believe that at the top of the hierarchy of gods are Brahma (the Creator), Vishnu (the Preserver), and Shiva (the Destroyer). Hindus believe that the human spirit is reincarnated many times, meaning that it is born into many bodies and lives many lives. Each time the soul comes to earth, it becomes more and more religiously pure.

Eventually, the soul becomes as pure as the gods themselves and enters Saccidandanada ("sach-ee-ahn-AHN-dah"), a state of perfect spiritual existence that requires no further incarnations. As the soul travels through these incarnations, it is classified according to its religious purity into one of four groups called *varnas* ("VAHR-nahs")—Brahmin ("BRAH-min"), Kshatriya ("SHAH-tree-ah"), Vaishya ("VAISH-yah"), or Sudra ("SOO-drah"). These *varnas* are ranked with Brahmin at the top. Within each *varna* are a number of subdivisions called castes. Although the caste system was not maintained among immigrants to Guyana, East Indians continue to recognize those born in the Brahmin group as the only legitimate religious leaders for their community. As the purist souls, only Brahmins can be *pandits* or priests of the Hindu religion.

Arya Samaj or Reform Hinduism was started in India in 1875 by Dayanand Saraswati. The main differences between the two sects are that the Reformists reject many of the practices of the Orthodox religion as superficial. For example, Arya Samaj Hinduism preaches that the three major gods, Brahma, Vishnu, and Shiva, are different facets of one god and that the minor gods are not gods at all, only humans who reached a high state of religious purity. For Reformists, worship involves meditation and yoga, rather than making offerings to idols or statues of the gods. The Reformists do not believe that a person is born into a *varna*. Rather, they argue that a person becomes a member of one of the *varnas* as a result of his or her actions on earth, so that a very virtuous person can become Brahmin.

A Hindu East Indian girl in Georgetown. Hindus believe that cows are sacred and do not eat beef.

73

Opposite: **Amerindian boys in Rupununi. Many indigenous groups in the Amazon and surrounding area have been forced to turn to Christian missions for protection from people coming into the area to exploit resources such as gold and diamonds. As a result, many Amerindian groups no longer practice their traditional religions.**

Below: **A group of Muslims in Georgetown.**

MUSLIMS A minority of the Indo-Guyanese are followers of Islam. Islam is a religion that was started by Prophet Mohammed in Arabia in the seventh century A.D. Islam has spread around the world, especially to the east, from its origins in the Middle East. Muslims believe in one God, Allah. Their holy book, written in Arabic, is the Koran. Muslim men attend prayer meetings in mosques.

Women do not enter mosques, although they also must practice prayer regularly. The Muslim holy day is Friday and Muslim holy men are called *imams* ("EE-mahms"). Although Hindus and Muslims in India have had a long history of ethnic strife and have even fought a civil war, in Guyana, relations are amicable.

OBEAH Some Afro-Guyanese practice a religion called *obeah* ("oh-bay-ah"). This is based on African beliefs and is related to voodoo in Haiti. Believers practice magic and believe that *obeah* priests have special powers drawn from traditional African gods and spirits. *Obeah* is based partly on the African concept that the ancestors have spirits that can affect the lives of the living and that relations between these two worlds have to be kept in good order. *Obeah* was made legal in 1970.

INDIGENOUS BELIEFS Among Amerindians there are a number of indigenous beliefs. Amerindians have been subjected to intense pressure from missionaries to convert to Christianity as part of the "civilizing" process. Sometimes this pressure has had disastrous consequences, as in the case of the millennial movement started by Awacaipu, a shaman of the Arekuna tribe.

Some groups have remained more isolated and have managed to maintain their belief systems. They have pantheistic religions. Mostly, the gods are represented by natural phenomena, such as waterfalls and animals like the jaguar. Amerindian religion stresses a respectful relationship between humans and the gods, who are evident in natural forms.

AWACAIPU AND THE COMING OF THE MILLENNIUM

Throughout the 19th century, European churches sent many missionaries to the Americas to try to convert indigenous people to Christianity. Often their influence was direct, in the form of missions established in the interior of countries such as Guyana. However, their teachings were sometimes indirectly powerful, as individuals carried their ideas back from trading posts or settlements. One such incident took place when Awacaipu, a shaman of the Arekuna tribe, returned from living in Georgetown. He had learned English and was very impressed by the teachings of the missionaries.

When he returned to his group, he told them of the coming of the millennium, an event predicted in the Bible. In his version, the millennium would bring the power of White people to Amerindians. When the time for the millennium came and went with no change, he told his followers to kill themselves so that they could be resurrected on Mount Roraima as "White people." When the dead people failed to reappear, the survivors turned on Awacaipu and killed him. Millennial movements such as this have been common wherever colonialism reached indigenous people whose lifestyle was radically different from the Europeans. The result was often that the indigenous people believed that Europeans possessed magic and that only through extreme practices such as suicide could they become like the Europeans.

THE HALLELUJAH RITE

As with Awacaipu, other Amerindians traveled to missions and learned about other religions. One of these, a Makushí from the savanna region, brought back stories at the end of the 19th century of a god named Papa (as in Father) who lived in the sky. He had a vision in which Papa told him to start a new religion called Hallelujah and spread it. Other groups picked up parts of the religion from the Makushí and one ritual, the thanksgiving ceremony, is still being practiced in the interior.

When hunters return with a good catch, they gather the animals and fish inside a hut that has been cleansed with water. Then they form a column outside the hut and begin to chant and drum to Papa, singing hallelujah. When they have nearly reached the hut, they form a line, each man with his hand on his neighbor's shoulder, kneel, and pray to thank the Papa spirit for giving them a successful hunt. This is clearly a combination of native and Christian elements. Ironically, when missionaries reached the interior, they failed to recognize this ceremony as part Christian and tried to ban it.

CULT GROUPS

Cults are religious groups that indoctrinate their members into total loyalty and obedience to their leaders. They can be very dangerous to society if their intentions are not honorable. Two such groups have unfortunately made Guyana their home in recent history.

Under the Burnham dictatorship, Guyana was home to two cults, both started by Americans. The more famous of these to the outside world was the People's Temple of Christ, led by Reverend Jim Jones. Jones brought the People's Temple to Guyana in 1974 with plans to set up an agricultural commune in the northwest of the country. Since this was territory disputed and possibly threatened by the Venezuelans and since Jones claimed to be a friend of Jimmy Carter, who would soon become president of the United States, Burnham allowed the People's Temple to buy land and establish themselves. The cult reached the attention of the media in 1978 when an American congressman, Leo Ryan, died in mysterious circumstances while investigating the cult in Guyana. Soon after, Jones convinced or compelled 914 of his followers to take cyanide in a mass suicide. Since even children were found dead, at least some members of the cult were murdered.

The second cult group is less well-known outside Guyana, but has had devastating effects on politics within the country. It was called the House of Israel and was started by "Rabbi" Edward Washington, a black American wanted by the FBI for a number of crimes, who fled the United States in 1972. His real name was David Hill and he convinced Burnham that he was a political refugee escaping a racist campaign against him. The cult was based on the belief that blacks were the original Jews and had the right to occupy Israel. Cult followers were indoctrinated to believe in the supremacy of blacks over other groups and to prepare for the day

Many of the followers of the People's Temple of Christ were black Americans, and Jones committed the full support of the cult to Burnham's dictatorship. Relations between the cult and the Guyanese government were dubious, as the cult was allowed to import drugs and arms with no interference from the authorities.

when other groups would be killed. There were about 8,000 members and they were protected from the law by their close ties to the PNC. Cult members wore uniforms that showed the colors of the PNC—black, red, and green. They were used by the government to disrupt legal strikes and to harass people perceived to be in opposition to the dictatorship.

On July 14, 1979, a cult member, Bilal Ato, killed an English Jesuit priest and photographer for the *Catholic Standard* newspaper, Father Bernard Drake, in full view of spectators. Burnham refused to investigate the murder and took three years to bring Ato to court, where he was defended by a state prosecutor and received a lighter sentence than demanded by his actions. Walter Rodney was one of the few who openly denounced the crime and accused the government of being behind it. The cult continued to function as long as Burnham lived. After his death, the government of his successor tried to soften the dictatorship and arrested cult leaders for crimes committed years earlier.

Under the cover of religion and dictatorship, these cults were given the right to operate in Guyana despite their illegal activities. The Guyanese people do not want a repeat of this situation in the future.

CHURCH AND STATE

Under the 1980 constitution, all Guyanese enjoy freedom of religion. There is no official state religion. Nevertheless, the major religious organizations have tended to associate themselves with political parties and have become quite involved in daily political life in the country. There are both Hindu and Islamic religious associations that have openly sided with both major parties, the PNC and the PPP, although the Indo-Guyanese have traditionally supported the PPP. The most vocal critics of the PNC dictatorship were the Christian churches and their umbrella organization, the Guyana Council of Churches (GCC). Today, with less political tension, church groups have been able to relax their pressure on the government.

FOLK BELIEFS

Besides formal religions, there are a number of folk traditions in Guyana. One in particular has captured the imagination of all ethnic groups. Stories about Anansi, a spider god from the Ashanti culture in West Africa, delight children of all backgrounds. Anansi, or Nancy as he is known in Guyana, is popular throughout the Caribbean. He is a trickster god, who is neither good nor evil. In the stories, he gets himself in trouble and using quick intelligence, manages to escape. One of his arch enemies is the tiger. Some have linked these stories to slave life, arguing that Nancy represents the slave, who is weak and must use cunning to survive, against the tiger or master, who is strong.

Folk traditions remain an integral part of the Guyanese people's lives. Nancy folklore is a powerful aspect of Guyanese moral life.

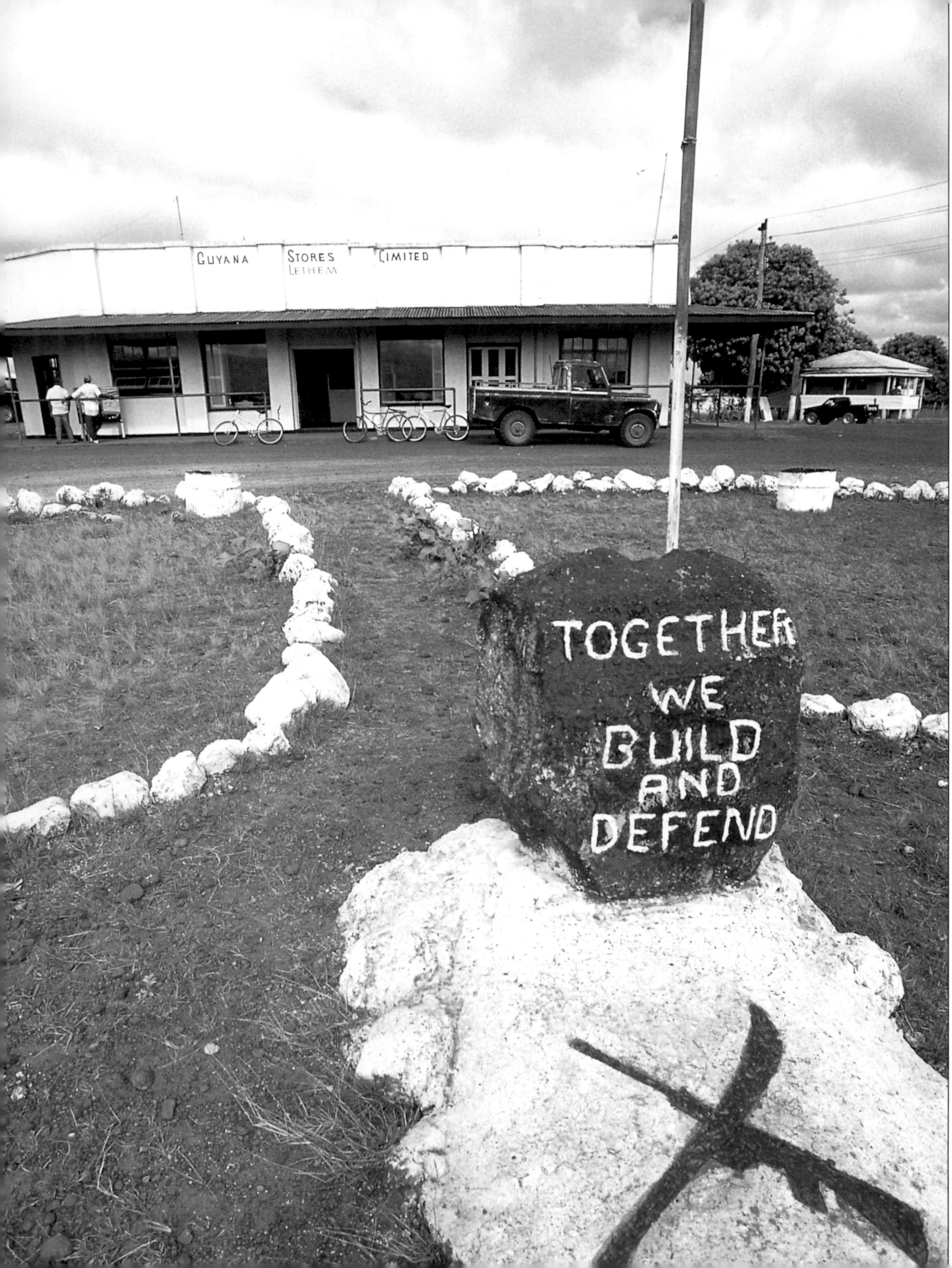
GUYANA STORES LIMITED
LETHEM
TOGETHER WE BUILD AND DEFEND

LANGUAGE

FOURTEEN DIFFERENT LANGUAGES are spoken in Guyana today, including some examples of a type of language called Creole. Many of these languages did not originate in Guyana, but over the years, they have come to reflect Guyana's unique human environment. In this chapter, we will consider how and why such a small country has so many different ways of communicating, as well as learn about different forms of communication such as proverbs and the media.

DIFFERENT LANGUAGES

English is the official language of Guyana, making the country an anomaly on the predominantly Spanish-speaking South American continent. As well as formal English, many other languages are spoken at home and in the streets. The majority of Guyanese also speak a version of English known as Creole, Creole English, or Guyanese. Creole is a language that

Opposite and left: **English is the most widely used and official language in Guyana.**

develops when people speaking different languages live in proximity and need to communicate. In Guyana, Creole English contains many influences from the other peoples and cultures that have contributed to Guyanese life and history.

For example, Dutch words that are still used today include *koker* ("KOH-ker"), which means watergate, and *stelling* ("STEL-ling"), a wharf or quay. Not surprisingly, these words describe things originally introduced and built by the Dutch. Although the French occupied Guyana for only a short time around the turn of the 18th century, they left a linguistic heritage in the word for rowboat, *bateau* ("BAH-toh"). Portuguese migrants have also left their linguistic mark in everyday language. Apart from some foods, there are also words like *briga*

WHERE DOES GUYANA BELONG?

Geographically, Guyana is part of the South American continent, but culturally and historically it shares more with English-speaking Caribbean islands such as Trinidad and Tobago. In fact, it is often classified with the Caribbean countries as part of the geographic region known as the Caribbean Basin. The reasons for this confusion in regional identity are many. To begin with, the Guianas (French, Dutch, and British) were the only non-Spanish and non-Portuguese colonies on the South America mainland. They are small and are dwarfed by their much larger Spanish and Portuguese-speaking neighbors, Venezuela and Brazil. When people think of South America, they rarely remember that not all of it is part of Latin America.

Its colonial heritage and modern linguistic and cultural makeup make Guyana "feel" more Caribbean than anything else, and this sense of identity is perhaps more important than the technicalities of geographic regions. In this way, language outweighs geography in giving the Guyanese their identity in the modern world.

Opposite: **An antispeed-ing campaign banner.**

("BREE-gah"), used to describe someone who wants to fight, and *olhado* ("ohl-YAH-doh"), which means evil eye. Chinese immigrants have mostly influenced the language with terms for food. There are dozens of Amerindian words in use, particularly as place names, since they were the first people to settle the territory. Other Amerindian words include *warishi* ("wahr-EE-shee"), which refers to a basketwork backpack, and *benab* ("BEN-ahb"), a hut. From the languages of India that made the voyage, words such as *typee* ("TY-pee"), a strong love, and *carahi* ("kah-rah-HEE"), a type of stewing pan, have entered everyday speech.

Some words from African languages have also come down through the generations, including *te-te* ("teh-teh"), a type of skin disease, and *kerreh* ("KEH-reh"), a state of power. Some common expressions in Creole English are "aw right," which means hello and okay; "me no know" to mean "I don't know;" and "just now," which can mean anything from right away to some time much later.

CREOLES: POST-COLONIAL HERITAGE

Areas such as the Caribbean Basin and the Guianas were ideal for the development of creole languages because so many people speaking so many different languages and dialects were brought together to work on plantations. While the dominant linguistic influence was that of the master class, workers of African, Asian, and other descent were able to influence the language used among themselves on the estates. For this reason, we talk of French, English, and Dutch creoles in the Guianas.

Because creoles are young languages, they often have relatively simple vocabularies. As a result, many people mistakenly assume that they are not true languages and undervalue their cultural significance. In fact, creoles are just as rich as more traditional languages and people speaking them can express the same range of meaning and subtlety as any person speaking a traditional language. Increasingly, creoles are becoming the language of post-colonial literature and thought in these countries.

Although English is the official language and Creole English is the language spoken by most people on the streets, other languages are still spoken in the home and within certain ethnic communities. A second creole found only in Berbice is a Dutch Creole left behind from many years of Dutch colonial occupation of the country. Sometimes just called Berbice, this language is nearing extinction as its speakers die. It is a combination of Dutch, a Nigerian language, and Amerindian. Another dying Dutch Creole is found in the Essequibo region and is known as Skepi. About half the words are similar to words in Berbice, but speakers claim that the two languages are not mutually intelligible.

In many Indo-Guyanese homes, you can still hear one of the two main Indian languages that were spoken by the original immigrants—Hindi and Urdu. These are the languages spoken by the majority of the people. The Amerindian minority also speak a number of languages and dialects based on the three main language/culture groupings found there—Arawak, Karib, and Warrau. Some specific Amerindian languages and dialects are Akawáio, Kalihna, Makushí, Patamona, Pemon, Waiwai, and Wapishana.

THE MEDIA

Most media in Guyana are directly owned by the government. Guyana Television Broadcasting Corporation provides limited service and supplements the two satellite relay stations that bring American television to Guyanese audiences. The Guyana Broadcasting Corporation (GBC) is the single radio station; it is also owned by the government. Once there was another station, Radio Demerara, but the government purchased it in 1975. The GBC currently broadcasts on two channels—GBC1 for the coast and GBC2 for the country as a whole. There are an estimated 398,000 radios in the country, and radio broadcasts are an important source of news and information for many people.

In the print media, the government owns the only publishing house, Guyana National Printers Ltd. It also owns the only daily newspaper, *Guyana Chronicle*, which it bought in 1974. There are other news weeklies and periodicals. The most significant of these are the *Mirror*, published by the PPP, the *Catholic Standard* published by the Catholic

VOICE OF THE PEOPLE: THE *CATHOLIC STANDARD*

Under the dictatorship of Forbes Burnham, all significant print media were controlled by the PNC or the PPP, with the notable exception of the *Catholic Standard*. This meant that there was only one public voice that tried to report the news accurately with no party bias. The paper was edited by Catholic priests, many of whom risked their lives to report and publish the news.

Many of these priests, particularly those acting as editors, lived with death threats and some, such as Michael James, assistant editor in 1979, were assaulted. Father Bernard Drake was killed while acting as a photographer for the paper in 1979. These men performed an invaluable public service, bravely bringing the news to Guyana and financing the paper with international donations. The paper is still published, but under much improved democratic conditions. It has a circulation of about 10,000.

The National Library in Georgetown.

Church, and the *Stabroek News*. The *Mirror* was, for many years, the voice of the official opposition to the dictatorship, as it represented the views of the PPP, just as the *Chronicle* directly reflected the views of the PNC government. The *Catholic Standard* was, until 1986, the only paper not linked to a political party. Under Burnham's rule, both these papers were harassed through accusations of libel and through limitations on the amount of newsprint they could purchase. Since newsprint is imported, the government could prevent it from being delivered to rival papers. Even donated newsprint was often denied to these newspapers.

In 1986, under Hoyte, a new paper was given permission to begin operations. Called the *Stabroek News*, it was printed overseas in Trinidad. The money for newsprint and other operating costs was raised in other countries—the first donation was made by the National Endowment for Democracy, an American foundation. It was printed weekly and shipped to Guyana. This marked a new beginning for relations between the press and the government.

FOLK WISDOM AND PROVERBS

One heritage that is particularly African is the use of proverbs in regular speech. With no formal education or writing allowed them, slaves used an oral tradition to pass on their cultural values. This is still evident today in the many proverbs that people use to communicate with one another. Proverbs are short metaphors that capture an essential idea about right and wrong or a story about how the world works.

An example of an Afro-Guyanese proverb, written in Creole English, is "Two hill doan meet but two men does meet," meaning that people can come together unlike immovable hills. Another example: if a parent accuses a child of doing one thing wrong and the child, out of guilt confesses to another crime, his parents will say, "Empty gun ah shoot guilty man," meaning that their false accusation actually caught him because he was guilty.

NAMES TELL A STORY

Guyana and its cities have gone by many different names over their long history. The basis for the name Guyana came from the Amerindian name for the whole region—Guiana. This word means "land of many waters," an accurate description of this area.

Georgetown has also gone by different names. Although it was founded by the English, the French were the first to name it, calling the settlement Longchamps. When the Dutch took it back from their French allies, they named it Stabroek, and the old town market is still known by this name. When the English took back Guyana for good, they renamed their colonial capital Georgetown after a British monarch. Inhabitants have also called their city Mudtown, which describes what used to happen to the streets after the seasonal rains. A map of Guyana shows the influences of various cultures. There are names left over from the Dutch and English, such as New Amsterdam and Queenstown, and others that have come from Amerindians, such as Roraima and Kaieteur.

ARTS

GUYANA IS A SMALL COUNTRY and has never been a rich one. This has limited the extent to which the government has been able to sponsor artistic activity. Nevertheless, there is a vibrant popular culture, complete with music and dance traditions from different ethnic groups and time periods. Literature has also thrived within the Caribbean tradition. Amerindians also contribute to the visual arts and crafts to make up a kaleidoscope of artistic possibilities.

VISUAL ARTS

Probably the oldest art in Guyana, the Timehri rock paintings are one of its most valuable Amerindian legacies. Located on a quartz cliff face near Imbaimadai (on the Karowrieng River, a tributary of the Mazaruni in western Guyana), they are a collection of roughly painted animals, symbols, and handprints that are believed to date back to A.D. 1300.

Opposite: **A Guyanese craft shop.**

Left: **Petroglyphs in Rupununi Savanna.**

Some of the animals portrayed include sloths, accurately painted upside down hanging from a vine, and anteaters. There are also abstract symbols such as squares, zigzags, and strings of lozenges (diamond shapes). At the base of the cliff, there are hundreds of handprints in red paint. There are so many of these that they overlap. Although these are clearly the work of prehistoric Amerindians, modern Amerindians in the area have a different story to explain Timehri. They say the paintings were done by their supreme god, Ama Livaca, who visited the area during a great flood. The paintings extend over an area 50 feet (15 m) wide and 25 feet (7.5 m) high and are so impressive that the name of this cliff was chosen for Guyana's international airport when it was renamed after independence.

Aubrey Williams, one of Guyana's best-known modern painters, also draws inspiration from the Amerindian past and present. He claims to have Amerindian blood and came to know the Warrau people quite well when he was assigned as an agricultural officer in their district. He spent two years with them and was even initiated into their tribe. His paintings reflect his knowledge of Guyana's interior, with its steamy primeval forests and powerful rivers. Other painters include Donald Locke and Denis Williams, who moved to Europe to paint and write.

ARCHITECTURE

Guyana's older cities and towns are notable for their distinctive architecture. The oldest and most valued buildings are all made of wood. The coast was originally forested, so there was an abundant supply of this material. However, pine was often imported for construction because it reacted to the tropical climate better than some of the locally available hardwoods. It was also easier to work when carpenters did not have power tools and was light enough to not sink into the alluvial mud of the coast.

In Guyanese housing design, the kitchen was always built in the back of the house in a separate, concrete-reinforced room. This was because wood stoves were the most common way to cook and presented a fire hazard in wooden homes. The demands of safety and a hot climate created typical Guyanese houses, which today are still an attractive feature of older sections of Georgetown.

HOUSING DESIGN IN GUYANA

As various generations of Guyanese adapted to living on the hot, humid, and flood-prone coast, a number of architectural innovations helped to make life cooler, drier, and safer. The first innovation in colonial housing was to copy local Amerindian designs and build the house on stilts. This kept it out of the mud and away from flood waters. The area beneath the house could be used for animals or storage. Houses, until very recently, were all constructed of wood. They were oriented to take advantage of the winds blowing from the northeast off the ocean. There were also special windows and shutters called Demerara windows. These are shutters that are hinged at the top and built out from the wall of the house. Between the shutter and the wall are moldings with decorative cut-out designs and at the base, a small tray.

   The holes in the moldings allowed for the passage of air, while the tray was used by wealthier houseowners for blocks of ice so that as the breeze blew over the ice, it would become cooler and thus cool the room inside. Ice was brought from North America and was stored in sawdust or sand until needed. The front of the house was dominated by a covered verandah that had shutters and jalousies ("jah-LOO-zees") to allow air to circulate. A jalousie is a system of louvers that can be differently angled. In this way, the whole wall was open to the sea breezes.

Amerindian-style archi-
tecture (foreground) in
Georgetown.

Guyanese houses were designed and adapted combining European styles and the demands of the local environment. Since stone or concrete construction would have sunk into the mud, even large public buildings had to be made of wood. Some incredible feats of engineering were accomplished in Georgetown. St. George's Cathedral, for example, is the second highest wooden structure in the world. Its spire reaches 132 feet (40 m) into the air.

This may not seem very high when one considers the concrete and steel skyscrapers of today, but to try to build something so high without a system of reinforcement (like steel beams) or a deep basement, is not easy. Guyana's colonial architects and carpenters, however, managed to overcome this difficulty. Although much of their work has been destroyed by termites and fire over the years, there still remain some impressive examples of this distinctly Guyanese art and craftsmanship.

MUSIC

This is perhaps Guyana's richest cultural treasure. All the different groups have contributed their musical sense and instruments to Guyana's national musical repertoire. For example, Portuguese immigrants brought both their *rajaos* ("rah-JOWZ," a type of banjo) and their *braggas* ("BRAH-gahs," small guitars) with them to the new land. One type of music that has been credited to them is *santapee* ("SAHN-tah-pee") music.

Probably the most common element in Guyanese music is the drum. Amerindian religious ceremonies, like the hallelujah rite, depend on the drum to set the rhythm and keep the beat. The Afro-Guyanese still use the drum extensively in a variety of musical forms. One of the more well-known types of music to come out of Guyana and other Caribbean countries is that of the steel band, which relies exclusively on percussion instruments or drums to make sound.

The Indo-Guyanese have also brought their traditional music and instruments, including the sitar *("sit-AHR"), a stringed instrument that is placed on the floor to be played because it is so long. Traditional Indian music is often played to accompany dancing.*

The Guyanese are quite active in the popular music scene. Eddy Grant (who scored an international hit with "Electric Avenue"), Eddie Hooper, and Sammy Baksh are all popular singers, while well-known groups include the Tradewinds, Traditional, and Mighty Kaieteur. The Guyanese contribution is most strongly felt in the vibrant Caribbean music scene.

Like many other Caribbean cultures, the Guyanese enjoy a wide array of popular music and dance styles. Dancing is one of the more popular activities among young people.

DANCE

As with music, Guyana enjoys traditional dance forms from many lands. The *kathak* ("KAH-tahk") is a traditional East Indian dance form performed by women. It is highly stylized and formal and requires years of training. The dancers are accompanied by traditional music.

Two distinctly African dances that made the crossing of the Atlantic and are still performed today are the *que-que* ("kwe-kwe") and the *cumfa* ("KUM-fah"). The *que-que* is performed by groups at weddings and other public celebrations. The group splits into two, with each side asking and answering questions about the people involved in the event. This can be quite humorous for the participants and spectators. *Cumfa* is a quasi-religious dance accompanied by drumming. The participants dance in a rhythmic fashion until they begin to fall into a trance. They believe that drums can summon supernatural forces and spirits that enter the bodies of the dancers. *Cumfa* is not performed as a public dance but in private among those who believe in the power of the drums and the dance.

CRAFTS

The Amerindian heritage and contribution is notable in Guyanese crafts. Indigenously-produced crafts include basketry, floor mats, and chairs made of woven reeds and grasses. Amerindian hammocks from the interior are also highly prized.

These remarkable creations are extremely light weight and can expand to incredible widths because of the natural fibers used and the technique of weaving. The sleeper can also use the extra material as a blanket so that the hammock becomes a complete bed. However, because they take a long time to make, most Amerindian weavers prefer to keep them for personal use.

An Amerindian weaver making *warishi* ("wahr-EE-shee"), or pack frame.

Other crafts produced in Guyana include brassware and gold filigree. Brass objects are made using a technique of beating or pounding the metal into shape. This takes not only skill but great strength and stamina and results in beautiful bowls and trays. Gold is also worked into filigree jewelry. Filigree work is the technique of rolling the gold into fine wires, which are then shaped into intricate designs and patterns. The work is painstaking and must be done by hand.

Some of Guyana's valuable woods are also used in furniture production. Both the green and purple heartwood trees make sturdy and beautiful pieces. The most highly-prized wood is wamara ("wah-MAH-rah"), a type of brown ebony that is very hard and durable.

Indigenously-produced crafts in an Amerindian building.

LITERATURE

The most significant trend in 20th century literature in the Caribbean and Guyana has been *négritude* ("nay-gree-TOOD"). This is a French word coined by Aimé Césaire, a black intellectual from the Caribbean island of Martinique. Césaire, along with other thinkers from Africa and Léon-Gontran Damas from Guyana, were students in Paris in the 1930s. This talented group was especially interested in the work of other black artists and writers and started a trend toward awareness of ethnicity and history in the arts. *Négritude* was a poetic term that was meant to stress the significance and beauty of black art from both Africa and the New World.

One of the writers that most inspired this group and their successors in the *négritude* tradition was René Maran of Guyana. Maran's novel, *Batouala* (published in 1921), was openly anticolonialist and written from the black viewpoint. It caused quite a scandal in literary circles but also won the Prix Goncourt in France. In response to the anticolonial debate surrounding Maran's work, the students formed an anticolonialist magazine called *Légitime Défense* (Legitimate Defense) that was published from 1932–34 in Paris. From then on, *négritude* and black pride were significant forces in the literature of the Caribbean. The most recent addition to the historical tradition of *négritude* was Guyana's Walter Rodney. His academic and journalistic contributions to Guyana were cut short as a result of his tragic political death in 1980.

Not all of Guyana's modern writers were influenced by Parisian culture. Edgar Mittelholzer sought the roots of his colonial identity in London, which he visited in the 1940s. His most famous work is *Morning at the Office*, published in 1950. Others, such as Denis Williams, found their inspiration and cultural roots in Africa. Williams is famous for his book *Other Leopards* (1963).

*Other writers from Guyana but not part of the tradition of anticolonialism include Wilson Harris, who has published two books based on the oral traditions of the Karib and Arawak Amerindians (*The Sleepers of Roraima, *1970 and *The Age of the Rainmakers, *1971) and a novel about travels to the interior during the colonial period in Guyana (*Palace of the Peacock, *1960).*

LEISURE

THE GUYANESE HAVE AN INTERESTING and unique approach to life that aims to balance work and leisure. Although most people are not wealthy, there are still many options for entertainment in the home and community. Family plays an important role in many leisure activities. The Guyanese also participate in sports and have inherited one of their most popular games, cricket, from the British.

MAKING LIFE

In the Guyanese language, a distinction is made between "making a living" and "making life." These two expressions refer to the two aspects of life that the Guyanese consider essential. The first, "making a living," has the same meaning in standard English and refers to working in order to provide food and other essentials for oneself and one's family. The second phrase, "making life," refers to socializing and taking care of other

Opposite: **An Amerindian family enjoying a game of cat's cradle.**

Left: **Socializing is a favorite leisure activity among the Guyanese.**

Young Guyanese enjoy a swim in the ocean.

members of the family and the wider community. Making life can mean anything from chatting with a neighbor to lending a hand when needed or participating in village or community events.

Both aspects of life, the economic and the social, are highly valued and the Guyanese strive to maintain a balance between them. It is considered unhealthy to focus so much on making a living that you ignore making life. People who are perceived to do this are considered to be greedy and antisocial. Likewise, people who only make life without working to make a living are called "limers" or are said to be "liming." This means that they are living off their friends and relatives and are not pulling their economic weight. There are a number of ways people make life in Guyana.

One of the most popular pastimes available to all Guyanese is going to the local store or marketplace to chat with neighbors. Older men with time on their hands, especially, will gather at popular spots in town to talk with one another. No other activity is necessary to make this a satisfying leisure activity. Younger men can often be found at bars, called rum houses, where they meet to share a drink and play dominoes. While women are not traditionally part of these male groups, they too meet to share the day's news, often at the market where they may be engaged in selling produce.

There are some ethnic differences in how people entertain themselves. For Afro-Guyanese youth, one of the most popular ways to spend a weekend evening is to go to a dance. Many villages have community centers where dances are held regularly, and towns often have mobile discos (movable sound systems) that can be hired for any event. Among East Indians, the tradition of public dances is not so popular because young women are not supposed to go out without a chaperon. However, people of all ages enjoy going to the cinema to catch the latest Indian movie. There is also a religious-based social event called a *jhag* ("JAHG").

Children at a playground.

HINDU THANKSGIVING AS A SOCIAL EVENT

At certain times in a person's life, there is cause to give thanks for the happiness and good fortune experienced. Hindus do not have a single thanksgiving day to do this. They can hold small family thanksgivings called *jhags* whenever there is a reason. For example, when a child is born and later has its first haircut, *jhags* are held by families who can afford them to celebrate and give thanks.

A *jhag* is nominally religious in nature, since a *pandit* is hired to read from the holy books and talk about religious matters. However, *jhags* are also social occasions when members of the extended family gather to socialize and celebrate successes in the family. *Jhags* can last up to five days and are accompanied by singing and feasting. They are as much social as religious and are part of making life.

SINGING ALONG FOR ALL AGES

The Song of Guyana's Children

Born in the land of the mighty Roraima,
Land of great rivers and far stretching sea;
So like the mountain, the sea, and the river
Great, wide, and deep in our lives would we be;

Onward, upward, may we ever go
Day by day in strength and beauty grow,
Till at length we each of us may show,
What Guyana's sons and daughters can be.

Born in the land of Kaieteur's shining splendor
Land of the palm tree, the croton, and fern,
We would possess all the virtues and graces,
We all the glory of goodness would learn.

Born in the land where men sought El Dorado,
Land of the Diamond and bright shining Gold,
We would build up by our faith, love, and labor,
God's golden city which never grows old.

Thus to the land which to us God has given
May our young lives bring a gift rich and rare,
Thus, as we grow, may the worth of Guyana
Shine with a glory beyond all compare.

In Georgetown, there are several more recreational options. The Botanical Gardens and the Seawall are popular for taking a stroll in the cool evening. Both of these public parks have bandstands where the Police Force and Defense Force bands sometimes play for the public. Georgetown also has a drive-in movie theater. People like to go early to have a picnic before catching the double feature. In addition, there are museums and theaters. Swimming in the ocean along the most populated stretches of the coast, however, is not popular because of the pollution from the drainage ditches and the silt from rivers and seawalls.

Children gather after school to play various games together. They especially enjoy activities such as kite-flying and simple games they make up. They may also play some of the sports popular in Guyana, such as cricket, field hockey, basketball, and soccer. Guyanese of all ages enjoy singing and music as part of their social activities. There is a large repertoire of popular songs and music, and even songs just for children or for parties. Story-telling is a traditional pastime that is dying out as more people turn to radio and television for home entertainment.

ANANSI AND HATE-TO-BE-CONTRADICTED

Hate-to-be-Contradicted was very bad-tempered and every time someone came to visit him, he would tell them ridiculous lies about his palm nut tree so that they would contradict him. When they did, he would hit his visitors with sticks because he hated to be contradicted. When Anansi came to visit, Hate-to-be-Contradicted played the same game with him, but this time the story had a different ending. Anansi agreed with Hate-to-be-Contradicted and told him a big lie of his own about his okra trees. Hate-to-be-Contradicted was going to contradict Anansi, but since he himself hated to be contradicted, he just agreed but said he would like to visit Anansi and see if the lie was true.

He arrived at Anansi's house and found all of Anansi's children telling him big lies about where their father was. This made Hate-to-be-Contradicted very angry, but finally Anansi came back. They fed Hate-to-be-Contradicted a stew with so many peppers that he cried out for water. One of the children went to get water but came back without any. The child said that he could not get water, because in the water jug, the water at the top belonged to his father, the water in the middle belonged to his aunt, and the water at the bottom belonged to his mother. The child said that if he did not take the right water, it would be sure to cause a fight. Hate-to-be-Contradicted got very angry with this ridiculous story and told the child he was lying. When Anansi heard this accusation, he ordered his wife and children to beat Hate-to-be-Contradicted, because although he hated to be contradicted, he had just contradicted someone else and therefore deserved to be beaten. They beat him until he shattered into little pieces which scattered across the land. That is why today, there are many people who hate to be contradicted.

SPORTS

By far the most popular sport in Guyana is cricket. This game originated in England hundreds of years ago and spread to most British colonies. The Caribbean colonies did not take part in the sport internationally until the 1920s, when the West Indian team was recognized as an international-class side in Britain. Guyana is one of the countries that has always contributed players to the West Indian team. Famous Guyanese cricketers include Roy Fredericks and Clive Lloyd.

Soccer and baseball are also popular in Guyana. Another sport played with a ball and stick is field hockey. Field hockey sticks are rather different

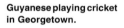
Guyanese playing cricket in Georgetown.

CRICKET, ANYONE?

Cricket is a ball and bat game popular in England and in former British colonies where children learned to play the game in colonial schools. The rules of the game are rather complicated and can be difficult for nonplayers to understand. Basically, the game is played between two teams of 11 players each. They play on an oval field called a pitch with two wickets, one at either end of the pitch. A wicket is a set of three posts or stumps in the ground on which are balanced two bails or shorter sticks. Each team tries to keep its bails balanced on the stumps throughout play. A bowler throws the ball and a batsman uses a paddle-shaped bat to try to hit the ball into the field. Unlike baseball, the batsman holds the bat quite low to defend the wicket that he stands in front of. If he hits the ball, he can score "runs," which are worth points in the game.

The batsman can be "dismissed" (similar to being "out" in baseball) from the game if the bowler hits the wicket with the ball; if a fielder catches the batted ball before it hits the ground (like catching a pop fly in baseball); if the batsman breaks the wicket with his own body or uses his body (instead of the bat) to defend the wicket; or if a member of the other team breaks the wicket while the batsman is attempting a "run."

Games are called matches and they can last for days since each inning is very long. An inning—there are only one or two in a match—ends when the 10th batsman is out, when a certain number of balls has been bowled, or when the batting team captain volunteers to end the inning. Players use padding to protect their legs from errant balls.

from ice hockey sticks and a ball is used instead of a puck. Field hockey is often played by girls as well as boys. Other sports that enjoy some local club support are basketball, rugby (similar to American football), tennis, swimming, and karate.

Horse racing is a popular spectator sport. Races in Britain are broadcast in Guyana and people love to bet on the horses. The local newspapers devote as much space to the races as they do to national politics. The Guyanese also like two other types of races—motor racing and goat racing. The Guyana Motor Racing Club holds international motorcycle and car races every March and October. Much less glamorous is goat racing, which is a local sport not found elsewhere.

A sport that attracts mostly foreigners is sport fishing. Although tourism is only now beginning to be promoted officially, the government has already acted to protect the environment and is discouraging the export of rare and endangered animal species.

FESTIVALS

BESIDES HOLIDAYS SUCH AS NEW YEAR'S DAY, Christmas, and Good Friday, the Guyanese also celebrate days that are important in their country's history. Hinduism and Islam also contribute official holidays to the list. Recognizing minority beliefs in this way serves to unite the Guyanese people in celebration.

CHRISTIAN FESTIVALS

The two most important celebrations in the Christian world are Christmas and Easter. Both are related to the life of Jesus Christ. Christmas marks the birth of Jesus and is celebrated on December 25 with family feasting and gift-giving. Easter, including Good Friday and Easter Monday, is a time to reflect on how Christ died for people's sins. Friday is the day he was crucified and Sunday is when he ascended to heaven. Although these are Christian holidays, everyone in Guyana participates in the festivities.

Opposite: **Young Guyanese celebrate New Year's Eve in Georgetown.**

Left: **Vendors at the beachfront in Georgetown enjoy their best business during public holidays.**

Christmas is one of the biggest celebrations in the country. Festivities are more numerous in the countryside than in the towns because people in rural areas have more time and know their neighbors well. Bands in costume called masquerade bands also travel through the towns. The music is accompanied by limbo dancers. Limbo dancing is a Caribbean favorite that involves trying to bend over backward to dance below poles held at various heights by other people. The best limbo dancers are true acrobats, since the objective is not to fall down or touch the pole. The music is produced by flutes and drums. People also visit each other's homes and wish each other Merry Christmas and Happy New Year.

Easter has become a time to enjoy such activities as kite-flying and country fairs. In Georgetown it has become popular to go to the Seawall to watch musical groups perform. As a four-day weekend, people enjoy the extra time to spend with families and friends.

Two clowns entertain a festive crowd. The week between December 25 and December 31, when the old year ends, is full of visiting and public festivities. It is as much a celebration of Christmas as it is of the end of the year and beginning of the next.

HINDU FESTIVALS

Holi Phagwah is the celebration of the new year and beginning of spring in India. It is similar in some ways to April Fool's Day because the festivities include trying to make people feel foolish by covering them with red- and yellow-colored powder and spraying them with colored or plain water. Kama, the Hindu god of love, is the deity celebrated at this time, which also makes it similar to Valentine's Day. For children, it is a fun time since they can spray people with water and powder in the streets.

Divali, also known as the Festival of Lights, is celebrated by Hindus around the world. It is a celebration in honor of Lakshmi, the goddess of wealth and prosperity. At this time, Lakshmi is said to return home from her summer residence in the mountains and lights are lit to help her find her way. Another reason for the lights is the story of an Indian king, Lord Rama, who was banished from his kingdom for 14 years. At the end of his banishment, he returned to reclaim his land, but it was the darkest night of the year, so the people lit up the night. Divali celebrates his return.

A Hindu temple in Rose Hall. The temple is the focal point for Hindus during religious festivals. Both the officially-celebrated Hindu holidays of Holi Phagwah and Divali are fixed by sightings of the moon at various times during the year.

MUSLIM FESTIVALS

Islam follows a lunar calendar with its own months. This calendar is not synchronized with the standard solar calendar, so important religious dates are not linked to the months of the solar year. This means that over time, these dates move, so they cannot be tied to regular seasons. The Islamic calendar marks a number of important days based on the life of the Prophet Mohammed—who revealed the teachings of the religion to the people—and other significant dates in religious history.

Religious practice in Islam is based on the "Five Pillars of Faith." These rules determine daily religious practice and inspire the major celebrations of the religion. The First Pillar of Faith is that there is only one true god, Allah, and Muslims must affirm this in their daily practice. This revelation was given to Mohammed on the "night of power," about ten days before the end of the month of Ramadan. This is celebrated in Muslim homes as Laylat al-Qadr. The Second Pillar of Faith is that Muslims must worship Allah five times a day.

The Third Pillar of Faith is that every Muslim must distribute charity to the poor. Although this can be done at any time of the year, there is a special celebration for it called the Feast of

Sacrifice, or Id al-Adha. This is one of the officially recognized Islamic holidays in Guyana. The Fourth Pillar of Faith is that all Muslims should fast during the month of Ramadan. This is the month when the Koran, or the holy book, was revealed to Prophet Mohammed. To show respect, Muslims do not eat or drink during the daylight hours. The family comes together to eat in the evenings. Id al-Fitr, or the Feast of Fast-breaking, marks the end of Ramadan. This is the most joyous family celebration in the Islamic calendar when everyone comes together to feast and celebrate the end of the fast. The Fifth Pillar of Faith is the *hajj* ("HAJ"), or religious pilgrimage to Mecca, a holy city in Saudi Arabia. Every Muslim must try to make the trip once in his or her life.

Though not related directly to the Pillars of Faith, Muslims also celebrate the day of Mohammed's birth, called Yum an-Nabi. This is also an official holiday in Guyana, although it is celebrated only within the Muslim community. There are special recitations about the life of Mohammed in the mosques and feasting among family members. A Muslim festival now dying out in Guyana, but one that was once the cause of interethnic strife in the countryside is the Tadja.

Opposite: **A Muslim man outside a mosque in west Demerara during the fasting month of Ramadan. Children under the age of 12, the sick, and the elderly are exempted from the fast since it could endanger their health. For those who practice it, it is a sign of religious devotion to avoid all food and water during the day.**

THE SACRIFICE OF ABRAHAM AND ID AL-ADHA

Muslims believe that the prophets of Judaism and Christianity are also prophets of Allah. They respect these prophets and the stories of their lives. One such man was Abraham, who was asked by Allah to sacrifice his son Ishmael (Isaiah in the Bible story) to prove his faith. He was ready to do this, but at the last moment, Allah told him to stop and provided a ram to be killed instead. Ishmael is believed by Muslims to be an ancestor of Mohammed, so this story is very important to them. To celebrate the day, Muslims prepare meat to eat together with their families and to give to the poor to represent both the sacrifice of Abraham and to fulfill the Third Pillar of Faith. This is also called the Great Feast, the Lesser Feast being Id al-Fitr to end Ramadan.

TADJA: UNITY OR DISUNITY?

This celebration is also known as Ashura or Hosay in other parts of the Muslim world. It is a ten-day series of events that marks the death of Hussein, one of Mohammed's sons. The culmination of Ashura is a procession that reenacts the burial of Hussein, complete with a replica of his domed tomb. Muslims carry the tomb around town, and if they are close to water, they may set it afloat. Tadja was once quite important in Guyana's villages, but this celebration often coincided with Hindu celebrations. When this happened, people often ended up in fights, as each group tried to push the other out of the way. The colonial government banned Tadja in 1930.

Since independence, it has been practiced peacefully with other groups participating, but is now in danger of dying out even among Muslims as the younger generations move away from the countryside and the traditional practices of their parents and grandparents. In other parts of the Caribbean, such as Jamaica and Trinidad and Tobago, Tadja is called Hosay and has become a celebration of East Indian, both Hindu and Muslim, unity.

Two international holidays celebrated in Guyana are New Year's Day and Labor Day. New Year's Day is the first day of the year in the standard calendar and is a time to recover from the festivities of Old Year's Night (New Year's Eve) and to enjoy family dinners. Labor Day in May recognizes the contributions of workers to the country.

HISTORIC HOLIDAYS

There are four major historic holidays in Guyana. The first of the year is February 23, which celebrates the founding of the republic on that day in 1970. This was when independent Guyana adopted a new constitution and declared itself a republic within the Commonwealth of Nations. Of all the historic holidays, this is the most festive. It is marked by such festivities as calypso contests, costume competitions, and picnics. Calypso is a type of Caribbean music where the words are quite important to the music. The highlight of the day is a parade of floats. Companies sponsor the building of floats that follow different themes, and these are then brought together for a parade in Georgetown that is judged for best float. Many people participate in the construction and decorating of the floats and many others come to watch the parade.

The next historic holiday of the year is May 26—Independence Day. This marks the day that Guyana became free of British colonial rule in 1966. Caribbean Day is celebrated in early July and is a time when people reflect on what it means to be part of CARICOM and the Caribbean cultural community. In early August, Freedom Day is celebrated. This commemorates the emancipation of slaves in 1838 and is celebrated by games and African drumming. People also eat African foods on this day to celebrate the African contribution to Guyanese culture.

A CALENDAR OF OFFICIAL HOLIDAYS

New Year's Day	January 1
Anniversary of the Republic	February 23
Holi Phagwah	February/March
Easter, including holidays for Good Friday and Easter Monday	March/April
Labor Day	May 1
Independence Day	May 26
Caribbean Day	first Monday in July
Freedom Day	first Monday in August
Divali	October/November
Christmas Day	December 25
Boxing Day	December 26
Id al-Fitr	varies
Id al-Adha	varies
Yum an-Nabi	varies

FOOD

THERE ARE AS MANY CUISINES IN GUYANA as there are cultures. Each group of people has brought something of their homeland and food preferences with them, and many of these "ethnic foods" have entered the standard repertoire of all Guyanese people.

AMERINDIAN TRADITIONS

Most of the Amerindian groups who still practice their traditional culture are horticulturists who clear small areas of land in the jungle to plant crops. Their staple crop is the cassava (manioc), a root crop native to the jungle. When cassava is raw, it contains prussic acid, which is poisonous to people. To remove the poison, Amerindian women first rub the root

Opposite: **A young vegetable vendor waits for customers.**

Left: **Fruits at a pier await transportation to the markets.**

across a board studded with sharp stones. This grates the hard tuber into shreds, which are then squeezed to remove the juice. The leftover pulp can then be ground into flour and used to make bread.

The bread is cooked on large flat pans over a fire. A flat bread, it does not contain yeast to make it rise. The poisonous juices are boiled in ceramic pots so that the poison is absorbed by the clay. What remains is one of the ingredients of Guyana's national dish, pepperpot. Pepperpot is a type of stew that also includes meat cooked for days over an open fire with lots of pepper. Cassava can also be used to make a type of alcohol called *casiri* ("KAH-see-ree"). The women chew the grated root, which is then allowed to ferment.

An Arawak woman makes cassava bread. Cassava is the staple food for most Amerindian groups, but they also hunt, fish, and gather fruits in the forest to supplement this diet.

Shoppers in a food store in Georgetown.

COASTAL CUISINE

About 90% of the Guyanese live in the settled coastal strip. The many different cuisines in this area are a reflection of the variety of cultures that live there.

EAST INDIAN   The East Indians brought their curries and *dahls* ("DAHLS") with them, and today many Guyanese count these as standard food in their homes. Favorite meat curries in Guyana are mutton, prawn, and chicken. *Dahls* are stews made with legumes such as lentils. These, like curries, involve the blending of lots of flavors and are cooked for a long time. The staple accompaniment to curry and *dahl* is rice.

A popular festive food is "cook-up," which is any kind of meat prepared in coconut milk and served with rice and beans. Coconut milk requires much labor to prepare and is very rich, so it is not eaten everyday in most homes. Another Caribbean food that reflects an East Indian heritage is *roti* ("ROH-tee"). These are large turnovers made with a flat bread and filled with curried meats and potatoes.

Shoppers in a food store in Georgetown.

117

CHINESE AND PORTUGUESE Both the Chinese and Portuguese have also contributed to the Guyanese menu. Guyana boasts of some excellent Cantonese restaurants run by its Chinese inhabitants. Noodle dishes are very popular. The Portuguese have contributed a variety of foods, including garlic pork, *bacelhau* ("bah-cah-LAU,"), *bolo do mel* ("BOH-loh doh MAYL"), garlic soup with egg, and *cus-cus* ("koos-koos"). *Bacelhau* is salted codfish and can be prepared in stews and soups. *Bolo do mel* is a cake made with molasses, a by-product of sugar processing.

Cus-cus was probably brought to the islands of Madeira from north Africa, where it is a staple food, before making the journey to Guyana. It is made from cracked wheat and can be flavored or plain. Pumpkin is used

Going out to restaurants is not as common as eating at home, but the Guyanese enjoy patronizing steakhouses serving up their own Rupununi beef.

as both a fruit and vegetable in Guyana, and the Portuguese fry it to make pumpkin fritters. As Catholics, the Portuguese observe Shrove Tuesday (the Tuesday before Good Friday) by eating special pancakes called *malassados* ("mah-lah-SAH-dohs") and *sonhos* ("SOHN-yohs").

AFRICAN The African heritage is also apparent in the use of yams and okra in many dishes, including *callalu* (see recipe). *Foo-foo* ("foo-foo") comes directly from Africa and is a type of cake made from plantains. *Metagee* ("MEH-tah-gee") is another coconut milk-based stew that includes yams, cassava, and plantains.

OTHER FOODS As a coastal country, seafood figures prominently in Guyana's kitchens. The best catches are shrimp, red snapper, and sea trout. All of these can be prepared in a number of ways and served with rice and peas. From the interior comes good quality beef and freshwater fish. Guyana also grows red and green peppers, green onions, eggplant, celery, avocados, tomatoes, and breadfruit.

A woman in Georgetown enjoys a meal of rice. For most Guyanese, the main meal of the day is at midday and most offices close around 11:30 a.m. to let their employees enjoy their lunch. A lighter meal is eaten in the late afternoon at around 5 or 6 p.m.

Opposite: **Stabroek Market in Georgetown. In smaller towns, there are general stores, marketplaces, and traveling vendors.**

DRINKS

As well as distinctive food, Guyana has several local drinks. The local beer, called Banks, has won many international awards. Banks is a brand that originated in Barbados, but is produced locally in Georgetown, too. A sugar-producing country, Guyana makes an excellent rum known as Demerara Rum. An internationally-famous cocktail was also concocted in Guyana. Called the Brown Cow, it is nine parts Tia Maria (a sweet coffee liqueur) and one part milk.

Children enjoy local soft drinks such as Banko Shandy, a ginger beer, and Malta. Guyana also grows a variety of fruits that make delicious juices, including oranges, grapefruits, pineapples, mangoes, tangerines, and watermelons.

RECIPE FOR CALLALU

This is a soup eaten as a main course that combines ingredients from land and sea. To make *callalu* ("kah-lah-LOO") you need the following ingredients:

2 onions, minced
2 celery stalks, chopped
3 tablespoons butter or margarine
1 ½ quarts (1.4 liters) water
1 cup (160 g) sliced okra
2 cups (320 g) chopped fresh spinach

1 ½ teaspoons salt
½ teaspoon dried thyme
dried chili pepper, a dash
½ lb (225 g) fresh shrimp, cooked
½ lb (225 g) ham, diced
½ lb (225 g) crab meat

Cook the onions and celery in butter for 2 or 3 minutes. Add water, okra, spinach, and seasonings. Cover, bring to a boil, and simmer for 10 minutes. Meanwhile, peel and devein the cooked shrimp. Add ham and shrimp to the soup. Simmer for 10 minutes more. Add crab meat to soup. Serve hot. Makes four servings.

SHOPPING

Every city and town has a central market where most people shop for their food and other household needs. The largest of these is Stabroek Market in Georgetown, which was built by the Dutch. Here, sellers and buyers gather everyday to haggle and bargain for food and other household supplies. Small producers of fruit and vegetables also ply the streets selling their wares or give them to children to sell after school.

Since many goods are imported into Guyana and therefore often in short supply, people try to develop good relationships with local shopkeepers. Sometimes, shopkeepers will refuse to sell goods that are hard to get to people who are not their regular customers or insist that the customer buys something else at a higher price in order to get the scarce product.

The North American routine of driving to the supermarket where everything is priced and in one place has yet to catch on in Guyana. Most people prefer to buy their food fresh and to shop frequently during the week. They enjoy haggling over prices. This system is also more environmentally friendly, since most food is not packaged and people bring their own shopping baskets rather than use plastic bags.

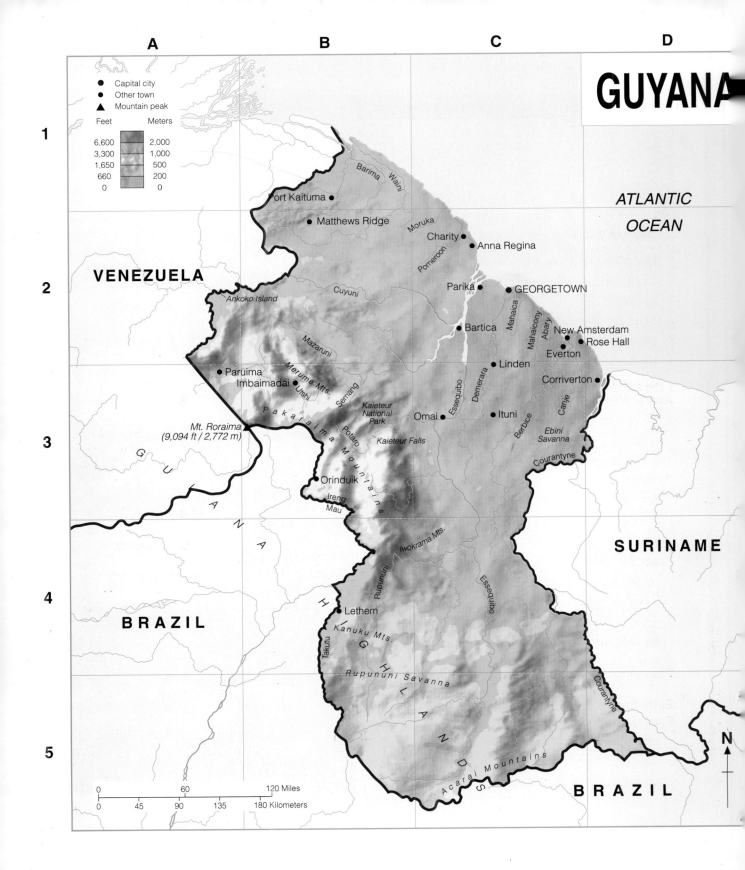

GUYANA

ATLANTIC

OCEAN

VENEZUELA

SURINAME

BRAZIL

BRAZIL

Capital city
Other town
▲ Mountain peak

Feet	Meters
6,600	2,000
3,300	1,000
1,650	500
660	200
0	0

Port Kaituma
Matthews Ridge
Barima
Waini
Moruka
Charity
Anna Regina
Pomeroon
Cuyuni
Parika
GEORGETOWN
Ankoko Island
Mazaruni
Bartica
Mahaica
New Amsterdam
Mahaicony
Abary
Rose Hall
Everton
Paruima
Merume Mts.
Imbaimadai
Ushi
Semang
Linden
Corriverton
Kaieteur
National
Park
Essequibo
Demerara
Canje
Mt. Roraima
(9,094 ft / 2,772 m)
Pakaraima Mountains
Potaro
Omai
Ituni
Berbice
Ebini
Savanna
Kaieteur Falls
Courantyne
Orinduik
Ireng
Mau
G
U
Y
A
N
A

Iwokrama Mts.

Essequibo

Rupununi

Lethem

Takutu

H

Kanuku Mts.

G

Rupununi Savanna

H

L
A
N
D
S

Acarai Mountains

Courantyne

0   60   120 Miles
0   45   90   135   180 Kilometers

N

QUICK NOTES

OFFICIAL NAME
The Cooperative Republic of Guyana

AREA
83,000 square miles (214,969 square km)

POPULATION
707,954 (1998 estimate)

CAPITAL
Georgetown

OFFICIAL LANGUAGE
English

HIGHEST POINT
Mount Roraima (9,094 feet/2,772 m)

LONGEST RIVER
Essequibo (630 miles/1,014 km)

MAIN RELIGIONS
Christianity, Hinduism, Islam

MAJOR TOWNS
New Amsterdam, Linden, Rose Hall, Corriverton

CLIMATE
Tropical with high rainfall and humidity

NATIONAL FLAG
Green, with a white-bordered yellow triangle (apex at the edge of the fly) on which is superimposed a black-bordered red triangle (apex in the center)

ADMINISTRATIVE REGIONS
Barima/Waini, Pomeroon/Supernaam, Essequibo Islands/West Demerara, Demerara/Mahaica, Mahaica/Berbice, East Berbice/Corentyne, Cuyuni/Mazaruni, Potaro/Siparuni, Upper Takutu/Upper Essequibo, Upper Demerara/Berbice

CURRENCY
The Guyana dollar
1 dollar = 100 cents
US$1 = G$143

MAIN EXPORTS
Sugar, gold, rice, bauxite, alumina, timber, rum, shrimps

MAJOR IMPORTS
Capital goods, consumer goods, fuel

POLITICAL LEADERS
Forbes Burnham—prime minister, 1964–80 and president, 1980–85
Cheddi Jagan—prime minister, 1957–64 and president, 1992–97
Janet Jagan—president, 1997–99

MAIN POLITICAL PARTIES
People's Progressive Party (PPP)
People's National Congress (PNC)

ANNIVERSARIES
Republic Day (February 23)
Freedom Day (first Monday in August)

GLOSSARY

Anansi
A spider trickster god popular in African tribal folk lore.

arapaima ("ah-rah-PAI-mah")
A freshwater fish that can grow up to seven feet (2 m) long and weigh 200 pounds (90 kg).

bragga ("BRAH-gah")
A small Portuguese guitar.

callalu ("kah-lah-LOO")
A soup combining ingredients from land and sea eaten as a main course.

capybara ("kah-pee-BAH-rah")
The world's largest rodent—also known as the water pig.

creole
A type of language based on two or more other languages.

cumfa ("KUM-fah")
A quasi-religious African dance accompanied by drumming.

jalousie ("jah-LOO-zee")
A system of louvered boards in Guyanese housing design that can be angled differently to allow air to circulate.

jhag ("JAHG")
A Hindu family thanksgiving, celebrated with religious talks, singing, and feasting.

Kali Mai Puja ("KAH-lee MAI POO-jah")
An alternative healing practice in Guyana.

kathak ("KAH-tahk")
A traditional East Indian dance performed by women.

négritude ("nay-gree-TOOD")
The focus on the contributions of black writers, artists, and thinkers.

pandit ("PAHN-dit")
Hindu religious expert.

pork-knockers
Men who spend their lives looking for gold and diamonds in Guyana's interior.

que-que ("kwe-kwe")
An African dance performed at weddings and other public celebrations.

rajaos ("rah-JOWZ")
A Portuguese banjo.

shirt-jac
Guyanese version of formal dress for men.

sitar ("sit-AHR")
A stringed East Indian musical instrument.

varna ("VAHR-nah")
One of four groups into which a soul is classified according to religious purity in Hinduism.

BIBLIOGRAPHY

Brill, Marlene Targ. *Enchantment of the World: Guyana*. Chicago: Children's Press, 1994.

Guyana in Pictures (Visual Geography Series). Minneapolis: Lerner Publications (Department of Geography), 1997.

Knappert, J. and Pelizzoli, F. *Kings, Gods, and Spirits from African Mythology*. New York: Schocken Books, 1986.

Rosen, Michael. *The Kingfisher Book of Children's Poetry*. New York: Larousse Kingfisher Chambers Inc., 1993.

Zaunders, Bo and Munro, Roxi. *Crocodiles, Camels, and Dugout Canoes*. Toronto: McClelland and Stewart Inc., 1998.

INDEX

INDEX